THE WASHINGTON NATIONAL CATHEDRAL
This Bible in Stone

This Bible in Stone

The memories of those who
prepared the plans
carved the statues
set the stones
designed the windows
played the music
and raised their prayers

to give substance to their faith
and joy to their commitment to create

A House of Prayer for all People,
The Washington National Cathedral
1907 - 1990

ROBERT E. KENDIG

Drawing by T. Tilghman Herring, Jr. AIA

THE WASHINGTON NATIONAL CATHEDRAL

This Bible in Stone

Robert E. Kendig

EPM PUBLICATIONS, INC.
MCLEAN, VA

Library of Congress Cataloging - in - Publication Data

Kendig, Robert E.
    The Washington National Cathedral : this Bible in stone / Robert
E. Kendig.
        p. cm.
    Includes index.
    ISBN 0-939009-91-9
    1. Washington Cathedral — History. 2. Christian biography-
-Washington (D.C.) 3. Washington (D.C.) — Church history — 20th
century. I. Title
BX5980 W3K46 1995   95 - 24820
283' .753 — dc20   CIP

EPM Publications, Inc., 1003 Turkey Run Road
    McLean, VA 22101
Printed in the United States of America

Cover and book design by Tom Huestis
Cover photograph by Robert C. Lautman

Maryland Window (inside front cover)
and Saint Peter Window (inside back cover)
by artist Rowan LeCompt

Foreword

We shape our buildings; thereafter, they shape us.

—Sir Winston Churchill 1960

Heinrich Heine, the 19-century German poet who studied the Gothic cathedrals of France and England as well as those of his native country, was asked by a friend why their age could no longer build such majestic structures. Heine opined, "In those days men had convictions, whereas we moderns only have opinions, and something more is needed than an opinion to build a Gothic cathedral."

Robert Kendig, the compiler of this volume, has spent ample time at the Washington National Cathedral—nearly a dozen years on the Building Committee and even more as a volunteer consultant to the Clerk of the Works—to realize that conviction was the motivating force behind the construction of our national house of worship. He was also privileged to overhear much opinion in his position, and realized that both elements comprised the remarkable history of the cathedral, an account which might be lost if not recorded for posterity. Thus, not long after the completion of the National Cathedral, he embarked on his own oral history project, first chronicling his mentor, Canon Emeritus Clerk of the Works Richard T. Feller, and thereafter Dean Emeritus Francis B. Sayre, Jr. and the other voices you will encounter in this book.

Future generations will be indebted to the industry of Bob Kendig for providing them with a deeper understanding of the participants—prelates, donors, architects, masons, artists and artisans, and worshipers of varied beliefs—who contributed to the conception, construction, and consecration of the National Cathedral. However, like any effective interviewer, there is hardly a trace here of the persistent compiler himself behind the notepad and microphone. What motivated Bob Kendig to compile this chronicle?

My own speculation is that Colonel Kendig developed an abiding interest in cathedrals when he was stationed in East Anglia as a United States Air Force flyer during World War II. In his spare hours between perilous missions, Kendig roamed the East Anglian countryside, that part of Britain which has the closest historic ties to our own country. As an amateur historian, he was enthralled by the looming majesty of the cathedrals he encountered. Who would not agree that the nearby cathedrals at Ely, Norwich, and Peterborough were among the most magnificent legacies of the civilization that the forces of democracy were then fighting to maintain? However, it was not until many years later, after a stint at the Pentagon and later as Director of Planning at the University of Maryland, that Bob Kendig turned in 1978 to offer his services to Canon Feller in the completion of the Washington National Cathedral. Thereafter, it was only natural that Kendig begin his oral history campaign by jotting down the recollections of Canon Feller. I suspect that Dick Feller, who is a natural storyteller in the tradition of his native West Virginia, needed little prompting. I am confident that the narratives gathered here will stimulate the memory of many others associated with the construction of the Washington National Cathedral. And no doubt Bob Kendig will be standing nearby with his notepad.

I am reminded throughout this volume of Samuel Taylor Coleridge's definition of Gothic architecture as "infinity made imaginable." These vivid stories of the participants in the creation of the Washington National Cathedral make their faith and their action altogether real and imaginable.

D. DODGE THOMPSON
National Gallery of Art
Washington, D.C.

Contents

Foreword
5

Preface
9

Stories from

THE VERY REVEREND FRANCIS BOWES SAYRE, JR.
13

RICHARD T. FELLER
36

RICHARD WAYNE DIRKSEN
69

JANE K. L. MILLER
80

ROGER MORIGI
93

JOHN H. BAYLESS
102

PETER CLELAND
118

LYN AND CARL TUCKER
124

A Miscellaneous Section
140

Glossary
171

Index
173

To Jeanne
who, for 47 years, has made coming home
an occasion to anticipate

Preface

Every culture has developed a literature of stories, legends and myths that serve to identify its customs and to color its history. Frequently stories attest to the values a society honors in its social and business associations. Stories become a part of the heritage. We shape the stories and then they shape us. They tell us who we are and what we believe. They describe the civilities we observe in our interchange with each other. They document the values we acknowledge in our relationships and associations. But sometimes stories merely entertain, and that is largely the function of the stories contained in this volume.

However, this is not what I intended to do. During almost 15 years as a volunteer associated with Richard T. Feller, the Canon Emeritus Clerk of the Works, and the one person who can be said to have "built the Cathedral", we enjoyed the anecdotes and stories with which he regaled us from time to time. Those stories, I believed should be preserved; for unless they were recorded, they would certainly be lost in time.

I suggested, that if he would use a tape recorder and tell me about the incidents, I would write the stories and they would be saved. He agreed. We were talking about perhaps three dozen stories at the most, but then the word got out as to what we were doing and there were others who also had incidents to contribute. They were accepted. Then still others were invited to participate. And look what happened!

Even if I wished to do so, it has not been possible to document all of the stories contained in this volume. The Cathedral Archives are both long and deep and, indeed, they have provided an authentication for many of the stories. Others do not lend themselves to that type of verification. They depend on memories, and frequently memories are inflationary.

All of the above to the contrary, notwithstanding, mistakes that may be discovered in the text are mine; I shall share them with no one. Try as one might, recounting stories such as those that appear herein is not an exact science. I absolve all contributors of any error and I prostrate myself in penance for all peccadillos.

Having said that, I presume that a modest amount of embellishment has occurred along the way. At least, there are many instances in which two or more persons recall the same incident in the same way. In other instances, the same incident is recalled differently, as if viewed from different vantage points. Living in Washington, as we do, that should surprise no one. I am reassured, however, in that in no instance did two or more persons recall responsibility for the same incident. That, in itself, is remarkable!

But to claim authorship for this volume is almost to perpetrate a fraud. There are so many who have given so much toward this effort that what they have recalled and told me has made it possible. In large degree, to record the names of these persons is to list the chapters that constitute the development of the cathedral. Introduce yourself to them now. You will meet them frequently in the stories that follow.

✦ JOHN BAYLESS. Beginning his work at the cathedral in 1930, he was one of the pioneers. He served the cathedral community as Business Manager, Curator, Boy Scout Troop Leader and in a host of other areas. He retired after 46 years of work.

✦ PETER "BILLY" CLELAND. The Master Mason who exercised standards of precision and excellence among the many masons working at the cathedral to see that the work was accomplished properly. One of the remarkable achievements of Cleland's time was the incredible record of safety that he maintained.

✦ RICHARD WAYNE DIRKSEN. Unlike the typical organist and choirmaster who relies on the published music available for religious services, Dirksen frequently composed his own. His compositions are so voluminous, in such variety and represent such diversity that they can easily overwhelm a lay person. It becomes something of an entertainment when traveling to see how many times one encounters compositions by Dirksen in far away cities and in other denominations. In the area of religious music, Richard Wayne Dirksen is truly a legend in his own time.

✦ RICHARD T. FELLER. Dick Feller was actively involved in directing all phases of the cathedral's construction for 37 years. A man of tireless energy, he as much as anyone must accept responsibility for the standards of excellence that have been followed in building the edifice. Although retired from daily activity with the cathedral in 1991, he continued to maintain an active involvement as the cathedral's art consultant.

✦ JANE MILLER. The Director of Visitor Programs and Volunteer Services, Jane is the newcomer to the group, having been with the cathedral little more than a decade. Possessed of boundless energy she constantly finds new things to do, new areas in which services may be expanded, new groups that may be served, new ideas to embrace.

✚ ROGER MORIGI. Roger served as the Master Carver at the cathedral from 1953 until his retirement in 1980. There are as many stories "about" Roger as there are stories "by" Roger. It was not possible to be around the cathedral and not know that he was also there. Roger was involved with everyone and everyone, who knew him became his friend. His friendship was endemic.

✚ FRANCIS B. SAYRE, JR. During his 27 years as Cathedral Dean, his intellect, commanding personality and leadership ability endeared him to all who knew and worked with him. Responsible for most of the iconography in the building, he also set much of the style that has been followed in its construction. For many Washingtonians, the name of Dean Sayre is synonymous with the Washington Cathedral.

✚ LYN AND CARL TUCKER. An active couple who spent 28 years in a multitude of activities at the cathedral, Lyn as secretary to Dean Sayre, buyer for the Cathedral Museum Shop, Executive Secretary of the National Cathedral Association. Carl as both musician and artisan extraordinaire, a man who worked in many media with notable results.

And it was Dean Sayre, in a presentation some years ago describing the iconography of the stone bosses in the vaulting of the nave, each carved to symbolize some passage of Holy Scripture, who said, "The cathedral is a Bible in Stone." It was he who supplied the title for this volume, not I.

If ever a person could be said to have been involved in a "labor of love," it has been I. One cannot walk through the cathedral day after day without being imbued with its majesty. One comes to love the building and I feel more blessed than most, for I have known many of the people who helped to make it. Not only do I see the many works of art and beauty, I sense the personna of my friends for they too are there.

ROBERT E. KENDIG
Washington, D. C.

September 1995

Aerial view by U.S. Army Air Service, 1923

The Very Reverend Francis Bowes Sayre, Jr.

Cathedral Archives

Although Dean Sayre retired from the deanship in 1977, he remains very active in the hearts, minds and memories of those of us still associated with the cathedral. A man of uncommon leadership skills and warmth of personality, probably more than any single person, Philip Hubert Frohman excepted, he shaped the character of the present day cathedral.

The grandson of President Woodrow Wilson, he was born in the White House in January 1915. His father was a professor at Harvard Law School, later an Assistant Secretary of State and diplomat.

His mother was Jessie Woodrow Wilson Sayre. He took most of his early schooling in Massachusetts, and graduated from Williams College cum laude in 1937. He spent the next two years at Union Theological Seminary in New York, transferring to the Episcopal Theological School in Cambridge, Massachusetts for his final year. There he studied under Professor Angus Dun.

After two years as a clergyman in Cambridge, Massachusetts, he became a chaplain in the U.S. Navy. He served from 1942 through 1945 and experienced some of the most rigorous naval campaigns in the Pacific. After the war, he went to Cleveland, Ohio where he served as an Industrial Chaplain for the Diocese of Ohio building a bridge between labor and the church, and management and the church. He became Rector of St. Paul's Church in Cleveland in 1947 and it was from there that he came to Washington in 1951 as dean of the Washington Cathedral. He was welcomed to that post by his former mentor, The Right Reverend Angus Dun, bishop of Washington.

During the next 27 years, the city of Washington was very much aware of his presence.

✦ Deeply troubled by the plight of the many refugees in Europe and elsewhere, he met with President Eisenhower and members of the Cabinet to discuss that concern. The scheduled six minutes became 45, with the result that additional millions of dollars in relief were committed to the cause.

✦ President Kennedy appointed him to membership on the nation's Equal Employment Opportunity Commission.

✦ In 1961, he did not hesitate to speak out against Robert Welch, the leader of the John Birch Society. Jointly with Bishop Garfield Oxnam of the Methodist Church and Dean James Pike of the Cathedral of St. John the Divine in New York, he inaugurated the first attack against Senator Joseph McCarthy.

✦ When the invasion of Cambodia occurred during the Nixon years, he earned the enmity of the White House by leading a march in opposition to this action.

Dean Sayre is possessed of a keen and contagious sense of humor that he enjoyed as much as those who experienced it. While serving as Dean at Washington Cathedral, he was urged on several occasions to be a candidate for election as bishop. He refused consistently. On one occasion, his reply included the following limerick:

> With election as bishop in sight
> (Which some seek with all of their might)
> For Dean Francis B. Sayre
> No episcopal chair.
> He would rather be Very than Right!

When he left the cathedral, he went to the Woodrow Wilson Center at the Smithsonian Institution as a Research Associate. After about 18 months, he went to Martha's Vineyard where he became Chaplain to the local hospital, a full ministry for ten years.

Dean and Mrs. Sayre, the former Harriet Hart, now reside at Martha's Vineyard from where we still, on occasion, receive a well placed remonstrance as well as a hearty chuckle.

The following stories are attributed to Dean Sayre.

It's a Measure of Faith

A French CEO of a large engineering firm, found it necessary to travel to Washington frequently during the early and mid-1970s, and on several occasions before boarding the Concorde for his return flight to France, he would come by the cathedral. Dean Sayre enjoyed showing the man around the building and explaining some of the more recent changes and additions to it. Always, the visitor would comment on the beauty of the building and the inspiration he experienced from the visits.

After several such visits, Dean Sayre asked the man, "Why is it that you find such pleasure in visiting Washington Cathedral? You have so many very beautiful cathedrals in France. Why is this one so meaningful to you?

"Yes", he replied. "We do have some beautiful cathedrals in France, but we have had them for centuries and we have become very accustomed to them. You are building this one now; and it is so reassuring to know that there is still a faith today that is strong enough to build a cathedral!"

The Dean had to agree; building a cathedral does require a measure of faith.

A Concrete Example

Washington Cathedral was built entirely by voluntary gifts and contributions from its many friends and visitors. Even though it had been the intent of our Founding Fathers to provide a large cathedral church in the nation's capital as "A House of Prayer for all People", no government money, either federal, state, or local has been used in the construction. Neither have individual churches or congregations been dunned to contribute to the cost, although many churches and civic groups have voluntarily given to the cost of the building and its program.

Frequently during the earlier days of his tenure, Dean Sayre could be seen escorting people through those portions of the cathedral that had been completed and showing them examples of the intricate carving of the limestone, the great care taken by the masons in construction, the concern of the architects and the care of the trades to create something approaching perfection. It was not unusual on these occasions to attract substantial gifts from the visitors who wished to participate in the construction of this Gothic cathedral.

On one such occasion, the Dean was showing a lady through the building who was known to be a person of substantial means. He showed her the ornate and beautiful carving of the limestone in the Canterbury Pulpit, the intricate designs of the limestone tracery in the windows, the sturdiness of the limestone arches and columns. She appeared to be duly impressed by the work that had been completed in the chancel, the choir, the chapels and north transept.

One can understand the dejection felt by the Dean when the lady on her departure, thanked him for the tour and remarked in all seriousness, that it was amazing what splendid things could be accomplished these days with concrete!

Photographing the Cathedral

Over the years, many of the persons associated with the cathedral either as staff or volunteers, have noted the vast numbers of people who visit the cathedral and persist in using their cameras with small flash equipment, presuming to take pictures of the interior of the building. Because of the enormous volume of space in the cathedral and the soft light, so that the stained-glass windows are more emphasized, it becomes almost impossible to obtain clear and distinct flash pictures. It has been suggested that in the course of time the value of under-exposed film used in the cathedral may begin to approximate the cost of constructing the building.

Some years ago the *National Geographic* magazine was doing a feature piece on Washington to celebrate the inauguration of a president. Every facet of the city's life was represented in superb photography. To represent the religious dimension, the magazine chose the cathedral, by that time completed some distance down the nave. They wanted to show the majesty of the building filled with worshipers. To that end they chose Easter.

Clearly, they would have to set the lights and wires in advance of the day. The only proviso that the Dean made was that they should not touch off the blaze of incandescence during the service, for fear of startling enough people to cause an ecclesiastical riot.

"By the time of the final blessing," said Dean Sayre, "I had forgotten all about it. I stood at the High Altar as the choir began to form for the recessional. I noticed a small commotion in one of our chapels alongside the Great Choir. A small but determined senior citizen was making her way through the crowd there. Her "Brownie" camera was in her hand; when she reached the dividing screen, she leveled her camera to catch the Bishop standing regally in front of the altar. Just as she pressed the button, the galaxy of light from the *Geographic* crew burst forth in a great flash of glory.

"The picture was a great full page in the magazine, but I couldn't help smiling as I caught the puzzled look on the little lady's face. She had no idea her small camera could rise to such an occasion. She went away mystified but happy."

The Vergers

The stone carvers had tremendous quantities of stones to carve. The problem that they encountered was that there was so much repetition. There were literally thousands of crockets and hundreds of finials, each of which was like all of the others that had preceded the one on which they happened to be working at the moment. For this reason, they liked the challenge of something different and something that would give them the opportunity to demonstrate the great sculptural talents that some of them possessed.

On the label moulds over the tops of windows and at the buttresses, each mould terminates usually with a carving of some plant, flower, animal or other representation that adds beauty, variety and interest to the edifice. A study of the many such terminations at the Washington Cathedral would be a fascinating undertaking.

There were two vergers in the 1960s who had been at the cathedral and who had served loyally for many years. Both of them were about to retire, and one had been hospitalized for a long time prior to his retirement. Dean Sayre wanted to memorialize both men and he chose a unique way. A stone carver demonstrated his talent by capturing the likeness of each man on the terminations of the label mould at the first window outside of the handicapped entrance on the north side of the cathedral.

James Berkeley and Edward Marr have both been captured in stone and are preserved for posterity.

Label mold terminations carved with the likenesses of Cathedral Vergers James Berkeley and Edward Marr.

The Pentagon's Cars

No matter how serious or solemn an occasion may be, there are always those instances in which the best efforts of the bureaucracy will contrive to introduce an element of absurdity. It happened at the funeral for President Eisenhower.

This was a State occasion and not only would the President and all members of the cabinet, justices of the Supreme Court and leaders of Congress be in attendance, but members of the diplomatic corps and many foreign dignitaries including heads of state. Someone thought it would be a good idea to have several cars with drivers standing by to take care of any visitor who might need transportation. The order was given at the Pentagon to have ten cars with drivers report to the cathedral and to stand by. Unfortunately, the clerk who wrote the order typed one too many zeros with the result that not ten but 100 cars showed up, all literally swarming around the cathedral to be available when needed.

The traffic jam was monumental. It went beyond gridlock. The dignitaries had difficulty getting into the cathedral for the ceremony and even the President's movements were greatly restricted. Several general officers attending the funeral, feeling the obligation to help restore order, went out to the driveways trying to move cars out of the way, but to no avail.

When the service was completed, President Nixon descended the wide steps of the north transept. There was his car waiting loyally to carry him off. But behind it came 100 tan sedans, eager to pick up some notable, none of whom seemed to appear. At last, a very high official ordered the cars to be off, and off they went, full throttle!

"I have wondered ever since that occasion," observed Dean Sayre, "what happened to that poor clerk who added the zero."

The Ethnic Angels

As the central tower of the cathedral was approaching completion, there was a requirement for the stone carvers to carve some 150 angels to be built into the four pinnacles. The angel heads would be interspersed with the usual crockets on the pinnacles and provide a relief to the tedium for the carver as well as the viewer. This was a very large undertaking.

Usually, when the carvers were to prepare a face, a sculptor would have completed a plaster model and the carvers would be able to follow it to produce the final stone carving. In this instance, however, the masons would need the carvings at an early date in order to set them in the pinnacles. The time available was so limited that some modification to the usual procedure was required.

After consulting with Dean Sayre, Mr. Feller met with the carvers and told them to carve angels as they thought the angels should appear. There would be no pattern for them to follow. Just as each carver had enjoyed full latitude in creating gargoyles, he was to have the same freedom to create his own angels. It would not have been possible to predict the result!

The carvers at that time came from a number of different backgrounds. They were from Italy, Greece, Yugoslavia, Scotland and there were several Americans among them, each of whom came from a different ethnic origin. As a result, the angels were carved reflecting a wide variety of ethnic features, in effect representing the nations from which the carvers themselves had come. Even though they are built into the fabric of the tower, hundreds of feet above the ground and not visible to the earth-bound beholder, the angels at the cathedral represent a veritable melting pot of humanity. What could be more appropriate for a cathedral built as "A House of Prayer for all People" in a nation that has welcomed all ethnic cultures?

The Lion of Britain

As Dean Sayre once observed, the construction of a cathedral is in many respects, a mirror of the times in which it was built. Every Gothic cathedral embodies within itself a reflection of the events of the day, both major and minor. This is substantiated at Washington Cathedral by an interesting happening.

During World War II, an Englishman who had completed some of the woodcarving in the choir stalls at the cathedral, passed away and left a notation in his last will that read, "My prediction for the end of World War II is to be found in the choir stall that I made for Washington Cathedral." The staff searched but could find nothing that would indicate such a prediction. They found what they presumed to be the Lion of St. Mark on the arm rest of the one choir stall the carver had completed, but there was nothing that seemed to indicate how this might predict the end of World War II.

"The Lion of Britain" with a serpent in its teeth.

Several days passed and one of the staff, looking more closely, noticed that there was a serpent clamped in the mouth of the lion, and upon close examination, the face of the serpent was clearly to be seen as the face of Adolph Hitler. The lion was not the Lion of St. Mark but the Lion of Britain!

A Nantucket Sleighride

Following the previous story, there is another interesting example of the construction at the cathedral that serves as a mirror of the times. This event was the carving of "A Nantucket Sleighride" that was recorded in the label mould terminations under the arches of the west balcony in the nave.

Dean Sayre had received four separate gifts for the cathedral that created an interesting situation. The four gifts came from four residents of New England; none of the four knew each other and all four were in some sense oriented to the sea. Why not combine the four gifts into a carving that was typical of New England and that would include a representation of that part of the country in the fabric of the cathedral? He did.

A sculptor was commissioned to prepare the models of four

separate panels that taken together constituted "A Nantucket Sleighride."

✠ The first panel pictures a dory, filled with harpooners and oarsmen going forth to find a whale.

✠ The second panel shows the lighthouse at Westchop on Martha's Vineyard.

✠ The third panel pictures the famous whaling mother ship, the *Charles W. Morgan*. This ship is now in a marine museum at Mystic, Connecticut.

✠ In the last panel, the whale has been harpooned and is attempting to get away, pulling the dory at breakneck speed. That is "A Nantucket Sleighride."

This piece of Americana is another example of what is included in the fabric of the Washington Cathedral that makes it truly a national shrine.

Origin of the Slype

Dean Sayre was in England visiting Durham Cathedral when he saw a sign that read, "Slype". He was intrigued since he had never seen the word before and he wanted to know how it was defined and what it referred to. He discovered that it referred to a covered walkway leading from the cathedral to the chapter house. Because the word could also be used in other settings, Dean Sayre on his return to Washington, employed the word to designate a roofed passageway between the north transept and the administration building where the business of the cathedral is managed. The area has become a room where clergy go to vest for services at the cathedral.

Well, to employ a word so erudite as 'slype', immediately connotes a degree of sophistication far out of the ordinary, and it bespeaks a level of urbanity and culture that would certainly impress the average visitor. The Dean was well pleased with this addition to the cathedral's lore until he walked by the refreshment area in the construction yard and noted that it had been christened, "The Slurp!"

The Rare Book Library

Shortly after his arrival at the cathedral, Dean Sayre planned a Sunday Service that would commemorate a special anniversary of the American Bible Society. For the occasion, he had facsimiles of many of the great Bible translations exhibited on tables in the Great Crossing.

After the service, Mr. Arthur Houghton, the donor of the Houghton Library at Harvard University came up to Dean Sayre and commended him on the service and his sermon and then added how unfortunate that he had to use facsimiles of the Bibles rather than to exhibit the real Bibles. The Dean responded that he had to work with what he had.

Shortly afterwards, Mr. Houghton returned with a gift for the cathedral. It was the King James Bible, from the first edition printed in England, that had been given to King James. He in turn gave it to his son, Prince Henry. The Bible came with the original binding and ties, dated 1611, and has been adjudged authentic. Dean Sayre was greatly impressed but he declined the gift, since he did not have the means to protect the Bible from fire, theft or other damage that might attack it. Mr. Houghton believed that the proper place for the Bible was at the National Cathedral so he gave the funds to build the Rare Book Library.

Today in the vault of that library is a wealth of gifts that have come to the cathedral: a copy of Archbishop Cranmer's Bible of 1572, an even earlier tome of 1551, and hundreds of other Bibles and Books of Common Prayer that make the cathedral Rare Book Library a repository of one of the most valuable collections of rare books to be found anywhere.

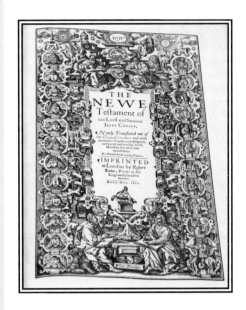

Title page of the New Testament *from King James' personal copy of the translation that bears his name.*

The Compression of the Vaulting

Sometime in the early 1950s, a stone fell out of the vaulting in the Bethlehem Chapel. There was no reason for it to fall and members of the cathedral staff were frightened by the happening. They were grateful that no one was hurt, but they wondered why a stone should fall out of the vaulting.

Mr. Frohman, the Cathedral Architect, was asked to explain. He had not been connected with the cathedral when Bethlehem Chapel had been constructed and he had to go back and study the "as-built" drawings to determine exactly how the construction had been completed. When he had satisfied himself, he returned to the Building Committee to tell them, "The vaulting in Bethlehem Chapel is not under sufficient compression; there is not enough weight on the vaulting," he said.

The committee had difficulty understanding this. There were thousands of tons of stone and concrete above that vaulting. But when Mr. Frohman explained, it became very understandable.

When the concrete had been poured over the vaulting in Bethlehem Chapel, in order to give the vaulting the weight it needed to keep it under compression, there was one principle followed by builders of 14th-century cathedrals that had been violated by the builders at Washington Cathedral. The violated principle was the law of gravity. Someone had thought that it would give the building additional strength to put steel reinforcing rods above the vaulting, in order to transfer some of the weight away from the vaulting and onto the walls. Just the opposite had occurred. There was not enough weight on the vaulting to enable it to do its job, to keep it under compression. The answer was to cut the steel rods, to transfer the weight from the walls to the vaulting.

The rods were cut. The compression created by the weight of the super-structure was transferred to the vaulting. The vaulting has performed perfectly ever since.

The Mosaics in Resurrection Chapel

The initial mosaic over the altar in the Resurrection Chapel, was completed by Hildreth Meiere, an artist of rare talent from St. Louis. As all who have seen the work will attest, it is a remarkable piece of artistry and beautifully accomplished.

When the cathedral staff was ready for the other mosaics along the sides of the chapel to be accomplished, the same artist was contacted and was given a commission to proceed with the work. She had barely started on the project when she contracted shingles and suffered greatly for a period of two years. Unfortunately, she was unable to complete the commission.

The cathedral needed artists to complete the last mosaics but could find none able to do so. Creating mosaics was rapidly becoming a lost art. It appeared that it would be necessary not only to create the mosaics but to create the artists as well. That is exactly what occurred.

Irene and Rowan LeCompt had demonstrated a remarkable talent to create stained-glass windows. The thought was suggested to train them in this art and commission them to complete the last mosaics in the chapel. Accordingly, the two were sent to Italy and to Constantinople to study the work of the mosaic makers from a former time. When the LeCompts returned some months later, they completed what is considered by some to be among the finest mosaics in America.

Spirits on the Tower

In any construction project, it becomes good policy to expect the unexpected. In that way one is less likely to be surprised.

When construction of the central tower had been completed, a little celebration was scheduled on top of the tower to include the persons who had participated and who had a part in either the planning or the execution of the construction. All were pleased to be a part of the observance. It represented the culmination of a major part of the cathedral's construction.

When the remarks had been concluded and the program was over, Dean Sayre was surprised to see the Linden crane descend to the ground and then to lift something to the top. It was a case of champagne furnished by the George Fuller Company, the General Contractor. With tongue in cheek, Dean Sayre suggested that this was the "greatest haul ever made by the Linden crane."

No one disputed him.

The Dean Can Also Demolish

Shortly after Dean Sayre arrived in 1951, he became aware that the Cathedral Chapter had attempted repeatedly to have the cathedral administration abandon and demolish several old cinderblock buildings on the close. These buildings had been used for a variety of purposes and seemed to be perpetuating themselves from year to year. In higher education it is frequently said that there is nothing so permanent as a temporary building on a university campus. The saying was becoming valid at the cathedral as well. No matter how often the Dean requested that the old buildings be removed, the staff could always find another use for them and clung to them stubbornly.

The new Dean had been in residence for a very brief period, not long enough to grow attached to the old buildings, but long enough to know that he held an obligation to the Chapter. He was athletically inclined and had spent some time on ranches in Texas as a cowboy. Accordingly, he not only knew which end of a sledge hammer one holds, he also knew how to wield the instrument, and people were stunned to see the Dean knocking substantial holes in the old buildings.

This implied that if what was in the buildings was of any value, it had better be rescued and moved. It was!

It also suggested that perhaps the buildings really might be torn down. They were!

It signaled that the new Dean might expect action to his requests. He did!

And so it was discovered, the Dean can build, he can also demolish. Be grateful for the presence of the Dean.

The Moon Rock

Every cathedral built in Europe is something of a kaleidoscope reflecting the times, the centuries in which it was built. Washington Cathedral is no exception. One can find many instances in the cathedral, in the stained glass, the stone carving, the wrought-iron screens that mirror the 20th century. One of the most popular of all of these examples is the Science and Technology Window—the Space Window—symbolizing the flight of Apollo XI, man's first journey away from Earth.

This event had to be reflected in the fabric of the cathedral. It should require a window that would transmit light both into and out of the cathedral, just as the trip to the moon involved two worlds. Dr. Thomas Paine, the former head of the National Aeronautics and Space Agency (NASA), understanding the need to provide the window, asked for the privilege to give it. A young artist from St. Louis, Rodney Winfield, working with all of the pictures provided from the trip of Apollo XI to the moon, designed the window as it is now installed.

While the window was being designed, a sudden inspiration came to Dean Sayre. Why not include one of the first pieces of the moon brought back to earth as a part of the window? So a request was made by the Dean for the gift of a small moon rock, a request that found its way to the White House.

During the Vietnam War, Dean Sayre had led a march in Washington, and had attacked the administration from the pulpit, protesting the bombing in Cambodia. This action was not regarded lightly by the Nixon White House staff and their memories were long. The request was vehemently denied.

Then began a long campaign of attempting to change opinions. A second request was submitted, this time in the name of Dr. Paine, with no reference to Dean Sayre. It did not go to the White House, but well down in the Federal Bureaucracy. After about a year, the Dean was asked by NASA to write a paragraph or so that would justify the moon rock being given to Washington Cathedral and not to some other church. But the memories were still long.

Bureaucratic mills grind very slowly. Eventually, Dr. Paine called the Dean to say he had received a letter from the President that authorized a gift of a slice of a moon rock to the cathedral. Of even greater interest, one of the paragraphs in the letter that President Nixon signed, was word for word, the paragraph of justification written by Dean Sayre. Even though memories remain long, they sometimes are distracted.

Shortly after the gift was authorized, the three astronauts from Apollo XI came to the cathedral and in a service of thanksgiving, presented the moon rock, four and one half billion years old, to be encased in the new window. It had taken a long time, but Apollo had finally landed.

The Theme of the West End: Creation

For most of the great cathedrals in Europe, the sinful nature of human kind, serves as the theme for a cathedral's west front. It has been chosen as the central theme so often that it has become almost universal. But at Washington Cathedral, it was decided to have the subject of creation serve as the west front central theme. It was believed to be more appropriate for the subjects of sin, redemption, and salvation to be manifested on the inside of the cathedral as one marches from the west end to the east end.

The crowning beauty of the west end is the rose window with the white glass at the very center that symbolizes God's creation of light—the separation of day and night—and His judging it to be good. This in turn is surrounded by the brilliantly colored glass, so that the colors playing on the fabric of the cathedral when the sun is on the window, create a rainbow, a re-enactment of God's covenant to human kind. But the interesting thing about this rainbow is that it moves as the sun moves. It does not stand still. It becomes a living covenant.

It is not merely the light that shines through the window into the edifice. In the evening, only a single light inside the building can reverse the sight lines, so that the cathedral shines out into God's creation.

The second representation of the theme of creation is, of course, the statue of Adam at the west central portal, the work of the sculptor Frederick Hart. Adam is seen as emerging from the stone that surrounds him but he is not fully formed. There is a reason for this. It is to say to us that God's creation is not fully finished but is a continuing process. Creation is an individual and personal experience for each of us, and it is played out over and over again for each person. As we discover new truths about our world, we experience new dimensions of creation. As we meet new friends and experience a new relationship with them, it is in a sense an act of creation. God's creation of the earth is a constantly emerging discovery for each of us. Creation, then, is a dynamic process. And humans have the unique opportunity of experiencing and participating in the creation of the earth each day.

Footnotes to a Career

A Ladder. After his mother had died, Dean Sayre admitted that he often thought of her as an angel who passed frequently between earth and heaven, performing ministrations of mercy for both himself and for others. Because this vision was so real for him, he gave a small stained-glass window to the cathedral in her memory. The window is in the turret stairs to the north balcony.

The subject? The window pictures Jacob's dream of a ladder in which many angels were continually ascending and descending, symbolizing a direct connection and relationship between heaven and earth, between God and a little boy.

Cesar Chavez and Ravi Shankar. September 28, 1969 was a day when we had two great groups at the cathedral. Cesar Chavez came to the cathedral in the morning with many of his followers. It was at the time of the labor troubles in California and the group wanted to have a special service that included Chavez, his workers, and many of those who sympathized with him. The cathedral was absolutely packed during their morning service.

The trumeau statue of Adam at the west central portal. The sculptor was Frederick Hart, the carver, Roger Morigi.

Photo by Stewart Brothers

That same evening, another memorable service was held in the cathedral. A memorial on the 100th anniversary of the birth of Mahatma Gandhi had been requested and arranged by the Embassy of India. The Foreign Minister of India was the principal speaker and Senator Eugene McCarthy also participated. Pandit Ravi Shankar came to play his sitar. Accompanied by Miss Kamala on her tanpura, he sat cross-legged under the Canterbury Pulpit and played a special number that he had composed for the occasion. His instrument provided a strangely haunting, yet beautiful concert to the audience of Hindus and their friends who were there for the memorial. Once again the cathedral was packed to its limits.

This is another instance in which the Washington Cathedral fulfilled its responsibility as "A House of Prayer for all People", by serving two very disparate groups of believing people.

To Facilitate Communication. When the central tower was completed, it was, of course, the highest elevation of any construction in the nation's capital, the only place where one could look down on the top of the Washington Monument. It was quite an occasion to climb those winding stairs all the way to the top of the tower and then to experience that breathtaking view of Washington.

During the administration of President John F. Kennedy, the federal government requested permission to install transmission and receiving antennae on the tower in order to facilitate communications with the President, no matter where he might be. In order to transmit and receive effectively, antennae had to be installed at a very high altitude and the central tower was considered to be the best place in Washington for this installation. When the Cuban missile crisis brought the Soviet Union and the United States so very close to armed conflict, the authorities agreed to install direct telephone communications between the President's office and the Chairman of the Soviet Union. The central tower also served this function for a number of years, until communications could be transmitted by satellite.

Establishing communications between adversaries does not guarantee a peaceful outcome, but it is very unlikely that peace will prevail without effective communications. In the final analysis, now that an agreement between the two adversaries has been achieved, it may be said that the central tower of the Washington Cathedral has truly been an instrument for peace.

A Man with many Hats. Each year during the first week of May the All Hallows Guild sponsors a Flower Mart on the cathedral close and there are tremendous crowds that flood in to experience the carnival atmosphere. Again in the fall, the cathedral sponsors an Open House and again large crowds come to celebrate.

On these occasions, the Dean was expected to attend. He did. It was also assumed that he would be dressed in his clericals. He was. Beyond that, however, it was not possible to assume what he might do. He enjoyed hats and on each occasion he would wear a different hat —a fireman's hat, a cowboy's hat, a Spanish hat, every occasion a different hat. Although years have gone by, people still remember the many hats he wore.

A Memorial to Helen Keller. There was a memorial service to Helen Keller in the cathedral and for this occasion, the Dean invited the choir from the Perkins Institute at Watertown, Massachusetts, a choir composed entirely of blind persons. There was no problem with the choir singing in the cathedral, but they were not accustomed to processing, as is the Episcopal custom. How could they process when they could not see?

The problem was solved very nicely. A sighted person led the procession that marched in single file, with each person placing a hand on the shoulder of the person in front. They were able to "see" their way through the processional, the service and the recessional.

A Visit from the Shah of Iran. The Shah had come to Washington on a diplomatic visit, not in any way associated with Washington Cathedral. His wife at that time, who had come with him, loved Gothic architecture and had become something of an authority on the subject. Accordingly, she persuaded the Shah to come with her for a visit to the cathedral where Dean Sayre gave them a tour.

They were eager to see some of the carving and masonry work that was being undertaken on the roof. There were two ways to get to the roof. A small elevator in the south transept would take six persons to the top. Other than that, one had to go up the spiral staircase in the tower, more than 200 steps and a tiring experience. Normally it would have posed no problem for all to take the elevator to the roof, but the Shah was attended by a dozen bodyguards. He solved the problem by announcing that the main party would take the elevator while the bodyguards would go up the stairway.

Shortly after they arrived on the roof, Dean Sayre saw the group of bodyguards emerging from the stairway, red-faced, breathless, disheveled, but rushing to the task of protecting the Shah. From the condition of the 12, the Dean saw little likelihood that any of them would soon convert to Christianity.

The Poor Boxes. For quite some time, the poor boxes that were installed to hold small gifts of money for the poor yielded nothing when they were inspected. None of the procedures for checking and controlling the boxes had changed. Why was there no income?

After a period of intensive investigation, the answer became clear. A member of the cathedral's security staff was the guilty party. The weakness of the human condition had manifested itself.

Inscribing a Name. Everyone enjoys seeing his or her name in print, provided the subject is a proper one. Dean Sayre was often approached by persons who wanted their names inscribed prominently as the donors of gifts. This was a difficult matter to adjudicate.

One such occasion was presented when the marble floor was installed at the great crossing. This would be a very expensive undertaking since different colored marble would come from all over the world. The donor wanted his name inscribed on the marble at the great crossing where his name would take pre-eminence over many of the saints and apostles.

The Dean pondered this matter and then informed the man that his name would indeed be inscribed at the crossing where it would be visible to God but not to man. It is on the under side of the marble floor.

A Bag of Gold Coins. A Verger came into Dean Sayre's office one day with a small bag of gold coins that had been taken from one of the several boxes placed to receive contributions. There was a brief note attached that explained the source of the coins.

During World War II, U.S. Army Air Corps pilots were required, on occasion, to fly over uncharted areas of Africa where civilization was only an occasional visitor. The pilots were given the coins so that if they were forced down, the coins might be used to expedite their return. Since in this particular instance the coins were not required, the pilot had given them to a lady who in turn gave them to the cathedral as a thank offering.

Moving the Glastonbury Cathedra. At the turn of the century, several stones from the ruins of Glastonbury Abbey in England had been given to Bishop Satterlee, the first bishop of Washington. The Abbey is historically significant to the Anglican Church and it was appropriate that the American branch of the church should have had these stones and that they should have been carved so as to constitute the bishop's chair. It is known as the Glastonbury Cathedra.

Shortly after his arrival at Washington Cathedral, Dean Sayre determined that the Cathedra had to be moved. It had been erected outside of the communion rail, a most improper spot for it. In addition, the triangular top of the chair was less than compatible with the curve of the wood screening above it. So the Dean said to move it. Moving a chair is no great task; you just pick it up and move it. In this instance, the job turned out to be somewhat more complicated.

✦ Because of the size and weight of the Cathedra, it had to be completely dismantled, stone by stone, and then reassembled at the new location.

✦ The place where it had been installed had no marble floor. New marble had to be installed after the architectural pattern for the floor had been completed.

✦ There was a door in the wooden screen behind the new location for the Cathedra. This had to be relocated.

✦ There were important electrical connections in the floor under the new place for the Cathedra and these had to be extricated and relocated.

To this day, Dean Sayre admits that he is hesitant to suggest to anyone, at any place, at any time that a chair should be moved.

Katharine Lee's Dog. Miss Lee was the Headmistress of the National Cathedral School for Girls and she had a dog that acquired a reputation of sorts. On one occasion it was guilty of biting a person coming into the school.

The incident has been preserved for posterity. One of the stone carvers has carved the dog in the upper reaches of the south transept with a portion of a man's trousers in his mouth. There must be some sort of message from this incident. The dog's memory will be preserved in stone for a millennium. Miss Lee, on the other hand, will soon fade from our memories and she never bit anyone.

The Sermon That Disappeared. When Dean Sayre was scheduled to preach at the cathedral, he always had his sermon placed on the lectern ahead of time so that as he was escorted to the Canterbury Pulpit by the Verger, he would not be encumbered by papers and manuscripts. It was always there awaiting him.

On one such occasion, he was preceded at the pulpit by Canon Wayne Dirksen who when he departed, accidentally picked up Dean Sayre's sermon with his other papers and took it away. For the average person, this would have meant a crisis of catastrophic proportions. For the Dean, it merely meant that he had to pull his copy of the sermon out of his sleeve and deliver it. He could not understand why others were not greatly impressed by this story. The reason was obvious. He seemed always to have something up his sleeve.

The Glastonbury Cathedra

Keeping other Peoples' Schedules. There were many different faiths and denominations that worshiped at the cathedral on a regular basis. One of Dean Sayre's most taxing duties was to keep the schedules in order. The liturgy differs greatly from one faith to another as well as the holy days of obligation. Unless all of these dates were coordinated closely, there could be real conflicts among them.

Among the many groups were:

+ The Polish National Catholic Church
+ The Syrian Church
+ Both Greek and Russian Orthodox Congregations
+ Periodic services by other groups

One Jewish congregation worshiped at the cathedral weekly for almost ten years. When they built their Temple and left the cathedral in 1958, they asked for a stone and were given a large ashlar, inscribed. It became a cornerstone in their Temple and remained in use as such for many years. Recently, a major renovation of the Temple was undertaken and the stone, that had not been really visable before, is now set in a ceremonial spot in the garden. It may be seen at Temple Sinai on Military Road in Washington. Like a proud parent that revels in the achievements of offspring, the Washington Cathedral may experience a sense of fulfillment in observing this active and vibrant congregation.

To Combat Demagoguery

In the early and mid-1950s, Senator Joseph McCarthy of Wisconsin, created a shocking and scandalous nationwide disturbance by making un-substantiated charges against individuals and groups of individuals, claiming them to be either communists or communist sympathizers. The term "McCarthyism" is now a part of our language, indicating those instances in which reckless and groundless charges are made that damage a person's reputation.

At the time that McCarthy first made his charges, it was, of course, politically correct for one to be completely and entirely anti-communist. The great majority of Americans were true and loyal to their country but they were fearful of being accused of being otherwise. And in the climate that existed at that time, it was not necessary that proof be presented; the charge was all that was necessary to render a person suspect. Then the person charged would be required to expend his own funds to employ legal counsel to prove his innocence. It was a frightful time and people were reluctant to make accusations of impropriety against McCarthy for fear of being targeted by the Senator.

Dean Sayre felt that "McCarthyism" should be exposed. He and two other clergymen, Dean James Pike of the Cathedral of St. John the Divine in New York, and Bishop Garfield Bromley Oxnam of the Methodist Church agreed to join forces to speak out against this evil. The three exchanged pulpits and spoke from Washington and New York.

This was not the kind of opposition that Senator McCarthy expected. He could not accuse the three of political motivation against him and it was the first time that he had experienced any organized opposition.

Eventually, in 1954 McCarthy became involved in a bitter controvery with the United States Army and he was subsequently censured by the Senate.

Competition for a Gargoyle

Gargoyles served a useful purpose in the cathedrals built in the early Gothic period in Europe. Since there were no gutters or down spouts available in those days, large amounts of rain would run off the roof, falling next to the building eroding the earth next to the building and, perhaps, damaging the foundation. By collecting the water on the roof and funneling it through gargoyles, the water would be directed away from the cathedral with great sound and fury. Our modern word gargle is a derivative of the word gargoyle.

At Washington Cathedral, gutters and down spouts dispose of all normal rainfall. The gargoyles will dispose of rainfall only in the event of an unusually heavy storm that is beyond the capability of the gutters to accommodate. So gargoyles at Washington Cathedral are primarily decorative, but they can be functional as well.

There is no standard form for gargoyles. They can vary from a representation of animal life to a grotesque that exists only in the artist's mind. In some instances, sculptors have prepared models that stone carvers followed, producing some very exotic gargoyles. Typically, however, stone carvers are given free rein to use their imagination with some amusing results. But when there were so many gargoyles to carve, the stone carvers had difficulty prodding their imaginations to produce a new and different pattern for each one.

In 1959, Dean Sayre, who always had a knack for involving people in projects, announced a competition for models of gargoyles. Anyone who wished to do so, could enter the competition and submit a model. The competition was announced by the Cathedral Public Relations Office with the thought that a few local people might find it interesting and respond. The announcement was picked up by several wire services and it appeared in the press throughout the nation.

The staff at the cathedral was dumbfounded! More than a thousand inquiries were received from persons asking for details of the competition and for the specifications to be followed. According to *Cathedral Age*, some of those responding were ". . . art students, a retired architect, employees of a TV station, a professional puppeteer, a contractor and builder, a 54-year-old woman draftsman and muralist, employees of an advertising agency, a college professor, public school teachers, a destroyer commander, a newspaper reporter and cartoonist, art schools and centers. . . and many others."

There were two problems associated with this competition that troubled Clerk of the Works Richard Feller. If the cathedral agreed to pay the freight for all models of gargoyles submitted, it would be paying to transmit tons of material to Washington. Clay and plastolina are heavy. It was decided to ask each applicant to submit several photographs of the model by which the jury could determine which models to have submitted.

The second thing that Feller noted was that almost all of the contestants were working on a work bench or a kitchen table and they spent great effort in carving and modeling the top of the gargoyle while the bottom of the model remained flat. He informed the applicants, "The only view of the top of the gargoyle will be by the Holy Spirit and pigeons. The top should be unworked so that rain will roll off and not settle on it. It is the bottom that will be seen from the ground and that should command your attention."

There were almost 100 contestants who took the contest seriously. Of these, the jury selected 15 to submit a model and of the 15 models, 12 were finally carved into gargoyles in the building.

Interestingly, some people took offense at the proposal to carve gargoyles and grotesques into the cathedral. They referred to this as a perpetuation of medieval superstitions saying that there should be no representation of evil in the edifice. Dean Sayre responded, "If there is no evil, then there is no need of salvation."

We Build with the Catholics

On a number of occasions, it became necessary, as Dean Sayre described it, for the cathedral to pause in its construction program and "catch its financial breath." One such occasion occurred during the 1960s, just when the Shrine of the Immaculate Conception had received a huge gift from the Knights of Columbus and was able to push on toward the completion of the basilica. There was one problem: their contractor could not find the highly qualified workmen required for the project.

The Dean called the Monsignor at the Shrine and told him of the hiatus that would be experienced at the cathedral and suggested that they might want to employ "our" people. It happened.

During the next several years, Dean Sayre would visit the Shrine and climb up on the scaffold to renew his acquaintance with "our" people. The completion of the work on the Shrine coincided with the renewal of work at the cathedral so that none of the workmen lost any time, and both edifices went forward to completion.

The Sacred and the Secular

In the cathedrals built in Europe during the 12th to the 14th centuries, that portion to the east of the rood screen or pulpitum, was the section of the edifice where religious services occurred. Consisting of choir, chancel, sanctuary, or by whatever name, this area was kept free of visitors. That portion called the nave, was reserved for the common people, and was used for a variety of purposes. In addition to religious services which might indeed be held there, it could also be used for business meetings, secular activities that were associated with the community, and on the occasion of great storms or even invasions by armies, the people might come to stay there with their families and many of their belongings, even bringing along their farm animals. Thus, this was no place for fixed seating and it was never provided.

The Dean was questioned about seating in the nave at Washington Cathedral and he announced that we would follow tradition and not have installed pews, but movable chairs. This has worked to the great good advantage of the cathedral where the flexibility of the open space has allowed a number of events to be accommodated.

In addition to religious services when chairs are set up for the worshipers:

✦ Booths and tables may be set up to display materials for distribution to visitors at various conferences or conventions.

✦ Exhibits and displays may be made available for examination during Open House observances or the Flower Mart.

✦ During the annual Diocesan convention held in the cathedral, tables and chairs are arranged so that conferees may have a light meal.

Pews are for parish churches and function well for them. Chairs that may be moved are for a cathedral.

The Queen was Tardy

When the War Memorial Chapel was completed, the Women's Auxiliary of the British Army asked for the privilege to complete all of the needlepoint kneelers for this chapel. They wished to make this gift as an expression of respect for the many Americans who gave their lives in two World Wars as comrades in arms with the British Army.

All of the arrangements were made through the British Embassy and in due course all of the kneelers arrived except one—Queen Mother Mary's kneeler, that was to be used in front of the altar, was not among them. This was noted with regret by the

Needlepoint Kneeler.
A gift from HRH, Queen Mother Mary.

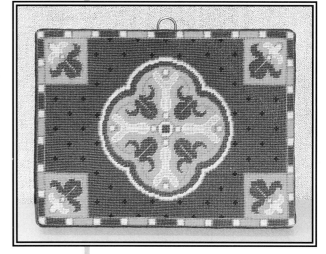

cathedral staff, but of course nothing was said openly about the omission.

When the time came to dedicate all of the kneelers, Queen Elizabeth II was here for the occasion. The service was held that expressed the gratitude of the Americans for this gift. As the party left the cathedral and the Queen descended the steps of the south transept to her car, she turned to Dean Sayre and said,

"Mr. Dean, I am so sorry. Mother just didn't complete her homework."

The kneeler did arrive before long and is among the prized possessions of the cathedral.

The Nixon Inauguration

In 1973 when President Nixon was planning his second inauguration, the planning committee announced that the National Symphony Orchestra would have a special concert and that the President had requested the orchestra to play the stirring 1812 *Overture* by Tschaikowsky. The purpose, of course, was to emphasize the commitment of the Administration to the conflict in Vietnam and the determination to see it through.

Dean Sayre believed that a significant emphasis should be made on peace rather than on war. Accordingly, he invited Leonard Bernstein to come down from New York and between the two of them they were able to persuade a large number of musicians, both instrumentalists and vocalists, to come to the cathedral to give a special concert. There were no fees; everyone was a volunteer.

With Bernstein conducting, a full symphonic presentation of Franz Josef Haydn's *Mass in Time of War*, was presented to a packed audience, overflowing outdoors. It was the largest crowd ever recorded to have visited the cathedral for any event. Members of Congress were in attendance led by Senator Edward Kennedy, Democrat of Massachusetts, and Senator Charles McC. Mathias, Republican of Maryland. Prelates of almost every faith and denomination were present. It was a way of bearing witness to sustain the conscience of a great many people who wished to emphasize peace rather than war at that particular time.

The Holy Eucharist was offered at 9:00 P.M. on January 19, 1973 at precisely the same time that the National Symphony Orchestra would be playing at the Kennedy Center.

The Visits to Selma

Dean Sayre often expressed his feelings about the mission responsibility that resided with a national cathedral. There were two directions that were open to it:

✚ It could avoid taking a position on social issues or on human rights and in so doing, become a rather empty, vacuous museum.

✤   It could fulfill his understanding of its need to address issues of justice and equity. A national cathedral should speak for the conscience of a nation.

The civil rights crisis that faced the nation in March 1965 tore at the fabric of social conscience and demanded that people take a stand one way or the other. It was not possible to ignore it. The issue was paramount and it would not disappear. Dean Sayre, the clergy and the staff believed that they had to take a stand and to dramatize their concern.

Two of the four clergy went to Selma to march with other marchers demanding freedom and justice for all Americans. They also visited churches in the area in an attempt to persuade them to support the effort. The other two clergy who remained in Washington went to the Capitol to lobby congressional delegations from the states that were in opposition. Then at mid-week, the four clergy changed positions so that all four eventually had a full range of experience in both areas.

On Sunday, March 14, the Dean decided that a statement had to be made from the pulpit concerning their experiences in the preceding week. He was sensitive to the fact that a report from any one of them might be interpreted as propaganda and not accorded the understanding that he wished the congregation to acquire. Accordingly, there was a corporate sermon in which each of the four participated. At the conclusion, all four stood there in the pulpit, united in their message, their belief, and their challenge to those in the congregation at the National Cathedral to see that freedom and justice would be guaranteed for all.

Richard T. Feller

Photo by Stewart Brothers of a painting by Eric Adkins

Richard T. Feller is a native of West Virginia who grew up in Martinsburg. He received a degree in Civil Engineering from West Virginia University in 1942 and spent the next ten years as an engineer in heavy construction before joining the Washington Cathedral in 1953. He was soon promoted to be Clerk of the Works, a position in which he was the administrator of construction and fine arts embellishment.

Feller has visited and studied all of the major Gothic cathedrals of England, France, Germany and Austria. At Washington Cathedral, he has directed the work of the architects, engineers, stone masons and stone carvers, as well as the stained-glass artists and wrought-iron artisans. In 1977, he became the first lay person to be appointed Chairman of the Cathedral Building Committee and in 1982 Bishop Walker gave him the title of Canon. Thus he became one of the first lay people ever to hold that title at Washington National Cathedral. In addition to being the "builder" of the cathedral, he is also its historian. He has written and published the history of the Washington National Cathedral through three editions.

Feller is rich with honors. He has been cited by the Washington chapter of the American Institute of Architects for his contribution to excellence in architecture. He was elected a member of the Cosmos Club in Washington. He is a member of the Most Venerable Order of Hospitalers of St. John of Jerusalem. More recently, he has been honored on three occasions by being awarded an honorary doctorate by colleges and universities, including his alma mater, West Virginia University.

Retired from the cathedral in October 1990 as Canon Clerk of the Works Emeritus, he continued a relationship with the cathedral's Building Committee, serving as an art consultant. He and his wife Billie maintain a home in Gaithersburg, Maryland.

South Transept Wrought-Iron Hinges

Jakob Schmidt, one of the foremost wrought-iron craftsmen with works in the cathedral, was born in a small town in the northeast corner of Italy in the latter part of the 19th century. From there he traveled to Russia before coming to Philadelphia where he worked in the studios of the great Samuel Yellin. Eventually, when his skills were recognized, he set up his own studio, and in the course of time he was commissioned to create the wrought-iron gate for the north transept stairway. When he completed the gate, he was awarded a commission to prepare ten pairs of hinges for the massive wooden doors at the south transept portal. Schmidt considered this to be one of the most important works of his lifetime, and although he was an elderly man and in failing health, he undertook the job with enthusiasm.

Shortly after beginning this commission, Schmidt lost his sight in one eye because of a cataract. The intervals between completion of sets of hinges became longer and longer and a second cataract left Schmidt almost completely blind, yet he was determined to complete the project. By the time Schmidt started work on the tenth set of hinges, his vision had deteriorated to such a degree that he had to depend on the sense of touch to guide him in his work. Although the cathedral representatives pressed him to complete the task, they did so with mixed emotions since they knew he would never have another project. It was suggested to him that it might be necessary to sub-contract the last set of hinges to someone else in order to complete the order, but he resisted this suggestion; it was his project and he wanted to complete it himself.

It took nine years for Jakob Schmidt to complete the ten sets of hinges and to deliver the last set for the south transept doors. He died shortly after completing this commission, knowing that he had fulfilled his obligation.

The Small Wrought-Iron Bishop

Jakob Schmidt completed another small but remarkable piece of wrought-iron artistry at the cathedral. In visiting Schmidt to observe the progress he had made on the south transept door hinges, Feller saw a very lovely, six-inch figure of a bishop that Schmidt had on display in his shop. He questioned Schmidt about the item. Schmidt replied that this was the piece he had prepared for the Guild in Italy to establish that he was qualified as a Master Iron Worker. When asked if he would sell the piece, he told Feller, "No, I could never part with my little bishop."

It was near the completion of his commission with the cathedral that Feller visited Schmidt and again noticed the little bishop. Schmidt had no immediate family, and he was unable to perform

The magnificent wrought-iron hinges at the south transept door that were crafted by Jakob Schmidt.

any further wrought-iron work. This time when Feller raised the issue, Schmidt replied, "I can't think of any place that I would rather have my little bishop displayed." He agreed to sell it to the cathedral and it was installed as a door handle on the inside of the door to the slype, the room that clergy use for vesting and that opens off the north transept.

The bishop/door handle is one of the great pieces of wrought iron installed in the cathedral, a piece of true museum quality.

The Frohman-Warneke Argument

Heinz Warneke, born in a small village near Bremen, Germany, came to the United States in 1923 and settled in St. Louis. He was a very successful sculptor and had a large following, especially on the East Coast. In the late 1920s he accepted an appointment as a faculty member in the art department at George Washington University and later became associated with the Washington National Cathedral.

Among several works of art in the cathedral, he was given the commission for the tympanum and the trumeau statue of St. Alban for the portal in the south transept. He met this obligation, completed the model and submitted it to the cathedral. Roger Morigi and Edward Ratti were the stone carvers assigned to transfer the model into the stone that had already been set for the tympanum and the trumeau statue.

In the tympanum, the two stone carvers began with the center figure of Jesus at the Last Supper and then worked in each direction to the right and the left. They had not gone too far when they suddenly realized that the model was not accurate. It was larger than the area of stone that was to be carved. It had not been kept to the same scale.

Master Carver Morigi notified both the artist Warneke and architect Philip H. Frohman. If the total model were to be carved into the tympanum, it would consume all of the stone area, even that portion that was to be left as the molding that contributes to the architectural and structural solidity of the stone work. Warneke was concerned with the integrity of his model and he believed that this was the only way to complete the work. Frohman, though sympathetic with the artist's point of view, was more determined to see that no compromises would be made in the building itself that might disfigure his design. A very heated argument developed between the two of them, each determined not to surrender his principles to the others.

Feller was called. He was still a newcomer to the cathedral, having been appointed as Clerk of the Works only recently, buthe knew enough not to try to mediate between two raging giants each of whom was trying to protect his own turf. Feller called for Dean Sayre.

Dean Sayre appeared, listened to the two appeals and proposed a compromise. He preserved the molding that the architect considered to be a mandatory requirement. Then by making some very minor changes in the dimensions of the model, everything fit in the space available and Morigi and Ratti very cleverly completed the carving.

Today, Feller cannot remember which part of the model was altered. It is not unlike many of the issues we feel constrained to defend with vigor. With the passage of time the point of the argument seems to escape us.

The Joseph Ratti Memorial

When Feller arrived at the cathedral in 1953, Canon C. Gardner Monks supervised all construction activities. Although a clergyman, he had previously been educated as an engineer and understood problems associated with construction. When Feller saw things that he believed should be brought to the attention of someone in authority, he would report the matter to Canon Monks. He warned Monks, in this regard, that stone carver Joseph Ratti did not observe good safety practices, in that he appeared to have no fear of height nor any thought of protecting himself when carving high above the ground.

Joseph Ratti was one of a number of Italian stone carvers who had worked at the cathedral. He arrived in the United States sometime in the 1930s and worked on a number of government buildings before he came to the cathedral. He had been employed on the Tomb of the Unknown Soldier and he had worked on projects at the National Gallery of Art. He was one of a number of stone carvers who worked on the lectern in the cathedral's Great Crossing and he also did carving on the north transept balcony.

Ratti was an excellent carver who worked effectively and efficiently but, as noted, he was inclined to be careless. In April 1955, he had been assigned to carve the gablet drip mould terminations for the first and second buttresses west of the north transept. When he had completed the second buttress termination carvings, he and a laborer began to move the scaffold planking to the first buttress. A single plank that was not sufficiently strong to support him gave way and he fell 40 feet to the triforium roof. Although he was moved very carefully in an ambulance, he died on the way to the hospital.

Feller decided the drip mould terminations would be left uncarved as a memorial to Ratti. No one knew how he would have carved the mould terminations, whether they would have been flowers, abstract designs or grotesques. As Feller expressed it, "Only

Drip mold terminations left uncarved in memory of Joseph Ratti.

Ratti knew how he was going to carve the terminations. It would have been improper for anyone else to attempt them."

And so they remain, two square drip mould termination stones, set in place, awaiting the carver's chisel that will never touch them.

The Washington Equestrian statue by Herbert Haseltine.

The Washington Equestrian Statue

The very first task Richard Feller was given when he was appointed as Clerk of the Works was to erect the George Washington Equestrian Statue that had been given to the cathedral.

James Sheldon had been one of the major contributors to the construction of Washington Cathedral. A major bequest in his will would provide the money that could build the central tower; but there was a caveat. Mr. Sheldon also had commissioned an equestrian statue of President Washington and he wanted it placed as near the cathedral's west doors as he could get it. Dean Sayre was reasonably agreeable to accepting the statue but he was less than enthusiastic about having it associated so closely with the fabric of the cathedral. A statue of our first president was wholly acceptable but not a statue that included a horse.

Dean Sayre and other cathedral officials made many trips to New York trying to resolve this issue. In his commission to the sculptor, Sheldon had specified that he wanted the horse's appearance to be based on Man of War, a famous race horse of the 20th century. Consequently, Washington is mounted on a horse that is probably far more pleasing in appearance than any he owned in his lifetime. But this was not a point of contention. The point at issue was where the statue was to be placed and Mr. Sheldon wanted it to be in a prominent place. The compromise solution was to place the statue in its present position at the foot of the Pilgrim Steps. The donor was satisfied with this location and the bequest of funds for the construction of the central tower was assured.

The sculpture had been commissioned to Herbert Haseltine, the well-known American sculptor who had also completed the sculpture in Arlington National Cemetery of General Sir John Dill, head of the British Joint Staff Mission to Washington, during World War II. The equestrian statue was intended to show General Washington on horseback on his way to church, although there was nothing specifically noteworthy about the sculpture indicating that the General was either going to church or pursuing some secular activity. Based on the description and the photographs of the work, however, it appeared to be a fitting bronze sculpture, dignified in its composition, that would be an appropriate addition to the close.

Dean Sayre and the Building Committee were eager to see the statue placed and did not wish to defer the matter unduly. An imposing pink marble base for the sculpture was approved and installed.

At the time the sculpture was commissioned, the artist was living in Paris and his studios were in that city. The sculpture model was completed in Paris, but it was cast in bronze at a location in Belgium and then shipped to the cathedral. It arrived in Baltimore encased in a large wooden crate and was then transported to the cathedral in an oversized truck. A large crane was brought to the close to lift the sculpture into position. When the crate was opened, the new Clerk of the Works was aghast to see that the statue had been gilded with gold leaf. It was not the bronze that the cathedral had expected. However, since the work had been commissioned, and since the crane was at hand, there was no alternative other than to set the statue in place in all of its gilded glory!

Several years following the final setting of the statue, it was learned that the elderly artist had failing eyesight and that the foundry studio in Belgium was very dark. In all likelihood, he had authorized the application of the gold leaf in order to give the work a sense of life and vibrancy that he had failed to see. There was correspondence with the artist proposing that the cathedral have the gold leaf removed, but Haseltine objected and, in fact, threatened to sue if that were done. The matter was dropped and with the passage of time, the cathedral authorities learned to avert their gaze from the gilded first president.

In the spring, the traditional graduation time when the sap rises in both botanical growth and male youth, it brings forth new leaves on trees and it also leads youth to escapades that they would not normally undertake. On one such occasion, the equestrian statue having been in place for some time, a graduating class at St. Albans School responding to this beckoning beacon, decided it would be an exciting adventure to apply red paint to the belly and legs of the horse. Immediately the school dispatched the appropriate service crews to remove the paint. The exercise commanded so much appeal, however, that two subsequent graduating classes at St. Albans proceeded to repeat it. After several years there was no gold leaf remaining on the lower extremities of the statue.

By this time the statue had become rather unsightly and since the artist had long since died, the Building Committee authorized the removal of the remaining gold leaf so that the original bronze of the statue would be exposed.

It must be admitted that gold leaf was not an appropriate treatment for our first chief executive. General Washington was a rugged outdoors man, a man of exalted position, but one much more appropriately shown in bronze. With the removal of the gold leaf, General Washington's dignity has been preserved.

41

Philip Hubert Frohman
and Cathedral Light Fixtures

Shortly after he was promoted to direct the construction of the cathedral in 1954, Feller was asked by Dean Sayre to improve the cathedral's lighting. At that time, the only permanent fixtures available were the very ornate and beautiful light fixtures installed in the Great Choir, which had been designed and fabricated by Walter Kantack of New York City. These Swedish iron light fixtures had been purchased in 1933 at a cost of approximately $6,000 each, an amount in those depression years considered to be exceptionally high. The same fixtures designed and manufactured in the 1990s, some 60 years later, might cost more than $50,000 each.

Typical of lighting fixtures designed and sold at that time, these fixtures were designed to reflect a Gothic sense of beauty by incorporating a number of flowers and foliage, but, conversely, they did not contribute much light. Some of the fixtures were moved several times and each time they were moved they were modified in an attempt to provide more light.

Aside from their poor light, no matter where the fixtures were placed, they interfered with the line of sight between seats in the nave and the reredos at the High Altar. Also, when the fixtures were designed originally, they had incorporated public address speakers in the centers to help transmit the spoken word from the pulpit.

When the early architectural contract had been drawn with Mr. Frohman, it stipulated that no appointment or furnishing was to be placed in the cathedral without his personal approval. This provision caused many anxious moments for Clerk of the Works Feller in his mediations between Frohman and the Building Committee.

Frohman was asked to design lighting fixtures for the nave outer aisles that could be used to increase the lighting level in the cathedral. Days, weeks and months passed, but no designs were forthcoming. After waiting for some time, Feller consulted a catalog of lighting fixtures and selected several that he thought might be acceptable in a Gothic setting. He asked Frohman to review them. After the architect studied the several selections, he responded to Feller, "I find it very interesting that no matter how bad the architecture may be, they have a light fixture to accompany it."

Feller subsequently contracted with a lighting consultant designer in New York, who both recommended the level of lighting necessary inside the edifice and also designed a number of fixtures that might be used. When the designs were available, Feller submitted them to Frohman in the same way that he would submit shop drawings of any materials or objects to be acquired, and asked the architect to make the corrections he wanted. Since this was a procedure that was familiar to Frohman, it worked effectively.

The Howard Kaiser Gates

Probably the greatest wrought-iron studios in the nation, early in this century, were those of Samuel Yellin's in Philadelphia. He had a number of fine craftsmen working for him and who were trained by him over the years.

One such artist was Howard Kaiser who began in the Yellin Studios as a water boy, serving the numerous craftsmen working with iron at the forges. Progressing over the years, initially as a novice and later as an apprentice, he became an outstanding craftsman and designer in his own right and continued working in the studio for many years.

In the reredos behind the High Altar, there were two openings to permit access to the area behind the reredos. As the years passed, it was decided to provide wrought-iron gates on each side to screen this area and to provide for security. Howard Kaiser, already in the twilight of his career, was awarded a contract to design, fabricate and install the twin gates. He made them similar in design but very dissimilar in detail. Kaiser wanted the gates to provide an effective contrast to the surrounding stone work. They needed to be dense enough to achieve the screening desired yet at the same time to provide a feeling of openness. His design was accepted by the Building Committee and the memorial gates were installed.

These two gates were the last contract Howard Kaiser ever accepted. When the contract was completed, he sold his tools to a young ironworker and retired.

South Transept Overcroft Floor

After the north transept and the Great Choir had been completed, Dean Sayre was impressed with the large amount of open space that was available over the stone vaulting and under the lead roof. While construction was halted on the south transept and a temporary roof had been installed at the triforium level, the Dean asked Feller about the possibility of installing a floor in the south transept over the vaulting to provide additional usable space for the cathedral.

An engineering study showed that a floor of reinforced concrete over the vaulting could be built. Plans were prepared and a floor was installed that included a very attractive small cloister at the south end of the floor. The space was designed with the thought that it might be an acceptable location for the Cathedral Chapter meetings.

With the installation of the ten bell peal in the central tower, and the requirement that bell ringers be available for long periods of time, a restroom became a necessity. A second engineering study established the feasibility of placing a restroom on this level by installing the plumbing lines in the elevator shaft of the south transept. At that time, the elevator had not yet been installed. When the restroom was complete, Feller warned the bell ringers to treat the facility with respect since it was the "highest level head in the District of Columbia."

Lastly, since the carillon had been installed, a place was required where the carillonneur could practice without disturbing the neighborhood. A practice room, containing a mock-up of the keyboard and pedals on the higher level was installed. On this lower level the carillonneur could rehearse in private.

There is no other known instance in which a Gothic cathedral enjoys an elevator in a tower or a transept rather than the usual spiral staircase with some 200 steps. Nor is there any other known Gothic cathedral that has a floor installed over the vaulting providing an overcroft with usable floor space.

Designing the Rare Book Library

Philip Hubert Frohman was beyond doubt a genius, a man of great vision, a man of exceptional design talents. But Mr. Frohman had his quirks. He liked to deal with the principal issue at hand and not with the ancillary things that were associated with it. Designing janitorial closets where one could keep mops, brooms, buckets and cleaning materials was anathema to him. He even was disdainful about providing a room where clergy could vest. He once told Feller his idea of hell was an eternity surrounded by mechanical engineers.

In working on his revisions for the west facade, Frohman chose to design a low, one-story structure beside each of the west towers in order to emphasize the height of the towers. The Rare Book Library was to be accommodated in the south structure that he designed, and it is a wonderful facility.

The main floor of the library opens into the Churchill porch and is equipped with display cases designed to show the rare books that are being exhibited and to show them to good advantage. The rooms are design exhibits themselves and they are well established to provide space for displays and special programs.

The lower level of the library contains a vault that provides security for the collections stored there. A significant collection of antiquated Bibles and Books of Common Prayer has been stored in the vault where the temperature and humidity may be controlled to provide the most desirable conditions for the preservation of old documents. The library has had an almost magnetic appeal to attract rare books to add to its collection. Frequently, selected groups of the many valuable books here are placed on exhibit for the public.

The Portable Organ

It has been said that Canon Richard Wayne Dirksen knew how to build an organ before he knew how to play one. However, he apparently had not heard the story of the man who built a boat in his basement that was too large to be removed through the door.

Canon Dirksen's father, a professional pipe organ builder, wanted to build an organ and give it to the cathedral. He knew how to construct them so that the result would be pleasing both to the ear and to the eye. It was agreed that he could proceed to construct an instrument and when finished, it would be placed in the St. Joseph of Arimathea Chapel.

The work progressed until the organ was finished and it was delivered to the cathedral. At that point, it became evident that the door leading into the chapel should have been measured before beginning the project; the opening was too small to receive the organ. As a result, the nave now has a portable organ in addition to the main organ in the Great Choir.

The Portable Organ built by Canon Wayne Dirksen's father.

The Nave or the Tower

After the issue of where to place the Washington equestrian statue had been peaceably resolved, the cathedral received one of the largest bequests that had as yet been provided. The construction of the two transepts had been completed, and now the Building Committee and the Chapter were faced with the question of what to build next, the nave or the central tower?

Opinions were divided as to what should receive the next impetus and there were good and compelling reasons for each point of view. Generally, the prevailing view supported building the nave in order to accommodate more worshipers at services and special functions. As several members of the Chapter said, "Building the tower would not provide a single additional seat." Then too, there was a precedent in New York, where at St. John the Divine Cathedral, they had built the nave rather than the symbolic tower.

Both Dean Sayre and Canon Feller favored building the tower but they were in the clear minority. Sayre believed that if the tower were constructed, dominating the skyline in Washington, it would bring in the money to build the nave. From a technical point of view, Feller knew that if the nave were built, the likelihood of ever building the tower with roofs exposed on four sides would be very remote. A further point with which all agreed was that the cost to build the central tower after the nave had been completed would be so much greater as to be prohibitive.

45

The issue was mounted and it had to be resolved. The Chapter would agree to the reasoning of the Building Committee so it was decided to bring the issue to that group for a decision. The architect, Philip Hubert Frohman, who was possessed of such a stature with the members of the committee that he was unlikely to be challenged, was invited to attend the meeting and to participate in the debate. He sat impassively, taking in the arguments on both sides of the question but saying nothing. Finally, he was asked by the Dean as chairman of the committee to state his preference. He replied very simply but directly, "I would build the tower."

The die was cast. The tower was built next.

The Linden Crane

In the mid-1950s, Feller went on an official trip to Bath Cathedral in England to obtain some additional information on cathedral construction. While there he saw a Linden crane, the first he had ever seen, and he was fascinated with it. To explain for the uninitiated: a Linden crane differs from other cranes seen around a construction site in that it is not mobile. The crane sub-structure is fixed, stationary, either in a location on the ground or in an empty elevator chase in a building. Once fixed, another crane is required to move the Linden crane. But it has several advantages over mobile cranes in that

+ it is more stable
+ it cannot tip over
+ it does not require street space and
+ it is less expensive to acquire and to maintain.

When Feller returned to Washington, he was enthusiastic in describing the merits of the Linden crane. He predicted that when it caught on, it would revolutionize the construction industry in this country, and he was correct. He investigated and found that there was only one such crane in this country, at Niagara Falls. The second crane came to the Washington National Cathedral.

The crane was used for all of the construction of the central tower and for the nave. When that construction had been finished, the crane was placed in storage. It was put into use again for the two west towers and served the cathedral until after the consecration exercises on September 30, 1990. It was sold shortly thereafter to a construction company in Texas.

One cannot estimate actual savings that may have occurred for the cathedral by acquiring a Linden crane, but a conservative estimate places the amount at more than half a million dollars.

Installing the Bells

In 1963, the cathedral experienced one of the great events in the history of its construction: installing the bells. The carillon bells had been cast by the John Taylor Company, a foundry in England that had been casting bells for seven centuries. The Whitechapel Bell Foundry that cast the "Big Ben" bell in the British House of Parliament had been selected to cast the ten bell ring.

The bells came by ship to Baltimore and were then moved by trucks to the cathedral. For the carillon, there were 53 bells and they varied in weight from the smallest, at 17 pounds, to the largest at 12 tons. The small bell was no problem, of course, but raising a 12-ton bell to the central tower was no minor task.

The construction crews had had experience lifting very heavy objects to the areas of their installation. Bosses, some weighing four tons or more, had been lifted to the level of the vaulting and then rolled to the final installation location by using round wooden rollers. It was decided to use this same system for the bells. Accordingly, a large, heavy duty wooden platform was built over the roof of the north transept. The bells were lifted to the platform, one at a time, placed on the rollers on the wooden runway and then rolled carefully into the central tower through an aperture that had been left in the north side.

When everything was in readiness for the crane to begin lifting the big bells, Feller ordered the cathedral to be evacuated. Several objected to leaving saying they could not see any real danger. Feller assured them that he trusted his engineer's calculations and he believed that the bells could be rolled into place with no danger, but he wanted to take every precaution.

"If any of you possess X-ray vision," Feller told members of the staff, "and you are certain that there is no weak member in any of our scaffolding, you may certainly stay in the cathedral during the installation of the bells." No one remained in the building but there was no untoward happening.

Mr. Frohman on Changes

Richard Feller never ceased to be amazed at Frohman's total concentration with the pure application of his architecture to achieve the perfection he wanted. He was determined to design a cathedral that would be the epitome of Gothic architectural perfection and to a large degree he was unconcerned with anything so mundane as money or the amount of it that was required to build the edifice. Feller learned very soon that if Frohman came to his office and spoke of changes he would like to make in the plans, he would submit a proposed five dollar change in the same tone of voice and with the same emphasis that he would use for a change of a much larger magnitude. Money was what other people worried about. He was building a cathedral!

Mr. Frohman was equally unconcerned about the symbolism that was embedded in parts of the architecture. Bosses could be carved to symbolize scripture, the creed or other manifestations of history or liturgical tradition, but once the boss was in place its architectural function had been fulfilled.

Dean Sayre and Feller had labored to assign the proper iconography of the bosses from the west end on to the great crossing and it had been a task to work out the parts of the Nicene creed to equal the number of bosses in the vaulting. It had been accomplished, however, and the stone carvers were busily engaged in carving those bosses that had been installed in the first bays of the nave. Everything had been worked out. Everything was in balance. There was complete agreement.

It was at this point that Dean Sayre left for the Far East for a six month sabbatical. And it was also at this point that Mr. Frohman came into Feller's office one day and began talking in general terms about the bosses over the west balcony. Feller was immediately alert. "There are no bosses over the balcony, Mr. Frohman," he said. "We have a barrel vault over the future west balcony."

"Well, I have made a change in the plans," replied Mr. Frohman. "A continuation of the pure Gothic concept in our architecture requires that we install vaulting ribs and bosses there."

Feller was aghast. What could he do? The Dean was away. He could not change the order of carving the bosses since many had already been finished. He could not re-write the creed; the church authorities would take a relatively dim view of that. Yet he was faced with 11 additional bosses that suddenly had to be included in the planned iconography and there were no statements for them. The Dean was responsible for the iconography, not Feller, but the additional bosses would completely destroy the order of things.

Difficult issues have a way of working themselves out. After much thought and study, it occured to Feller one could very well say that the creed was based on the foundation of the ten commandments. When the Dean returned, he agreed with Feller's recommendation.

Today any visitors studying the iconography of the cathedral bosses, would be persuaded that the organization is indeed brilliant. The assignment of ten boss stones over the west balcony to symbolize the ten commandments (with the 11th and largest of them carved to symbolize Moses holding the stone tablets) looks as if it had been planned from the very beginning. Neither the Dean nor Feller would suggest anything to the contrary.

The Monjo Angels

Enrique Monjo, a prominent sculptor of Barcelona, Spain was given the commission to sculpt the 44 angels in the south transept portal tympanum. Monjo's work was well known in Spain since he had completed many commissions for multiple figures in a confined setting in Spanish churches. He had also trained his stone carvers to work with pneumatic hammers, something almost unheard of in Europe at that time.

Monjo could speak no English and neither Feller nor Dean Sayre spoke Spanish. Both the Dean and Monjo spoke acceptable French, however, so all of the communication concerning the south transept was conducted in a diversity of languages. The Dean and Monjo spoke to each other in French; Sayre translated to English for Feller while Monjo translated to his assistants in Spanish.

There were 44 angelic figures to be carved into the portal voussoir and eight life-size figures to be placed in the niches below, four on each side. Monjo wanted to prepare his plaster cast models for all the figures at his studio in Barcelona. He also wanted to use his carvers to fashion the eight life-size figures and then ship them to the cathedral. Feller was skeptical about this, but he knew that the artist would be more comfortable in his own surroundings so he offered no objection.

Monjo returned to Barcelona and began work. It was necessary, of course, to have formal acceptance of the work by the cathedral's Building Committee in order to pay Monjo. There was only one way this could be done; Feller on behalf of the Building Committee had to travel to Barcelona, inspect the work and certify that the quality of the sculptures was acceptable. The eight large statues were completed as well as the 44 angel plaster models, each one different, all with life and vitality. The 44 were later carved into stone *in situ* by the cathedral's carvers, Roger Morigi and Frank Zic. They have become a beautiful part of the south transept portal.

Four and a half years were required to complete the 44 angel figures. Feller considers the voussoir one of the great accomplishments in 20th-century stone carving.

49

President Wilson's Canopy

When President Woodrow Wilson died in 1924, it was arranged that he should be interred at Washington National Cathedral. At the time, only the Apse, the Great Choir, and Bethlehem Chapel, which was on the crypt level, had been constructed. Accordingly, the President was interred temporarily in Bethlehem Chapel with the understanding that his casket would be moved eventually to the nave. In 1972, the construction of the nave had progressed to the point that his tomb could be transferred to its permanent resting place.

In order that the original temporary tomb be accorded the dignity it deserved, Dr. Ralph Adams Cram had been asked to design a handsome wooden canopy for the site in Bethlehem Chapel. When the casket was transferred to its permanent place in the Wilson Memorial Bay of the nave, the ornate canopy was no longer needed.

The wooden canopy for President Wilson's temporary tomb. Designed by Dr. Ralph Adams Cram.

On the north side of the nave in the first north aisle bay west of the north transept, opposite the Wilson Bay, a lighted cabinet was installed to contain the Books of Remembrance listing gifts given to the cathedral as memorials as well as the memorial books of needlepoint gifts in the chapels. The Wilson Canopy was altered to fit the area and installed over the cabinets. It has, thus, served two very remarkable functions. It has served to honor the memory of a great president who first suggested an international commitment for the nation, and to honor those who helped build and embellish the nation's cathedral.

The Navy Pilot Memorial

Persons who make gifts to the cathedral come from many diverse backgrounds, with many different intentions, for many different purposes. Regardless of the size of the gift, each one is taken seriously. And when it appears most likely that a gift must be refused, something seems to happen to prevent any disappointment.

Feller was working in his office one day when a woman from Cleveland, Ohio came in saying that she wanted to give a memorial to her son. He had been a Navy pilot, had been killed in combat in World War II and had been buried in Arlington National Cemetery. A widow of very modest means, she had saved her money for ten years to provide for a memorial at the National Cathedral. Further, she wanted the memorial to be carved in stone. It was obvious that she had no idea of how expensive stone carving was; she had accumulated only $250. Yet as impossible as the situation appeared to be, Feller was determined to try to accommodate her and to provide some type of memorial.

Trying to stall for time, he invited the woman to walk into the cathedral with him. He knew he would be unable to find an uncarved stone anywhere that could be carved for $250 although he felt a deep sense of urgency to meet her need. As they walked into the south transept, Feller looked up and saw a small label mould termination, that in all of the years he had been at the cathedral, he had never noticed before. He knew at that instant that the stone had been placed there to be available as a memorial and this was the occasion. He pointed out the stone to the woman and said to her, "I believe this stone will meet your requirement and I am convinced that it has been saved for you." She was elated!

Feller said a quick, silent prayer of thankgiving and sent the woman on her way home content in the knowledge that she had been able to provide a carved stone memorial for her son at Washington National Cathedral.

It has been so recorded.

Fire in the Cathedral

The carillon, including the steel framework to support the bells in the central tower, weighs about 150 tons. Obviously such weight requires a very substantial support, so a heavy concrete floor with a massive reinforcing network of iron bars was installed to accommodate it. As is usually the case, heavy plywood treated with oil had served as the base on which the concrete floor had been poured. When the concrete was hardened and the wooden forms had been dismantled, the sheets of plywood were stacked under the new concrete floor until they could be removed from the tower.

Clerk of the Works Feller returned to Washington from an out of town trip and, as was his custom, called home to tell his family that his flight had landed. His son answered the telephone and greeted his father with a very cheery, "Dad, what did you think about the fire at the cathedral?" Feeling that the earth had been cut from under him, Feller took a taxi to the cathedral as quickly as he could get there.

Fortunately, he found the fire not to be a serious one. A workman had failed to extinguish a 300-watt light bulb when he left for the weekend and the light had rolled on to one of the plywood sheets. The heat from the bulb was sufficient to ignite the wood. The only lasting damage was that the smoke stained the under side of the new concrete floor and it is still black to this day.

Memorial to a Navy Pilot. Sculptor, Carl Bush.

Photo by Stewart Brothers

Dean Sayre reported an interesting experience with one of the firefighters. The Dean was standing in the nave helping to direct the firefighters to the elevator in the south transept that would take them up to the overcroft and thence to the site of the fire. At night, with only a few lights burning, the cathedral is indeed awe inspiring, if not downright intimidating. One of the firefighters, fully clothed in his protective coverings and carrying a fire extinguisher, running from the north transept entrance to the south transept elevator, caught sight of the dimly lighted High Altar from the Great Crossing. He paused, genuflected, crossed himself and then continued on his run.

Lighting at the Crossing

The story of attempting to provide adequate lighting in the cathedral is a continuing saga. One of the more interesting lighting problems developed as a result of televising services from the cathedral. This constituted a novel use of a cathedral church since no such service was ever anticipated when the building was planned and the requirement for a massive amount of lighting was foreign to the very nature of a cathedral.

In the 1940s, the television networks began coming to the cathedral to broadcast services that would have a wide appeal to the American public. Special memorial services or funerals of dignitaries and the special Christmas service came to be anticipated by the public. Accordingly, networks planning to televise these services would appear well in advance of the occasion, employing dozens of technicians to install the temporary special lighting.

As one might imagine, technicians installing lights would be far more concerned with having the proper level of light to eliminate the darker nooks and crannies than they would with the care of the cathedral's stone work. Frequently there was damage to the triforium and columns where lights were improperly affixed. This resulted in the cathedral staff's taking precaution to prevent damage, frequently creating tension with the television lighting crews.

Before he became a U. S. Senator from Virginia, Secretary of the Navy John Warner, a member of the Cathedral Chapter became interested in the problem of accommodating the television crews. The problems could be obviated by installing permanent lights so that they would not normally be visible from the nave floor but would provide an adequate level of lighting when required.

Fortunately, this need arose at about the same time liturgical changes in the Episcopal Church resulted in moving the celebration of the Eucharist from the traditional High Altar to a movable altar set up at the Great Crossing between the nave and the transepts. This action moved the celebration to a more central place in the church, where it was surrounded by the people rather than remote from them. Since the crossing was the primary area that needed to be lit, it was far more convenient to use its four corners at the triforium level as the places where lights might be installed. When the lights were not in use, the mechanisms could be retracted so that they were not visible.

A generous gift was secured by Secretary Warner to pay for acquiring and installing the lights. Initially, the lights were installed on movable tracks that were extended manually from the triforium. At a later date, electric motors were added so that the lights could be extended or retracted automatically. Rheostats were also installed that made it possible to control the intensity of light.

Television crews still prefer to use their own lights that they bring with them for services to be televised. The new lights are still used in varying degrees for nearly every service, however, since the participants have grown accustomed to having them.

Hearing the Spoken Word

The 20th-century cathedral has been greatly influenced by the development of technologies in new and emerging fields. Public address or sound systems were not available during the cathedral's earliest construction; indeed, electronic sound amplification was virtually unknown.

During the mid-period of construction, in the 1940s, a sound amplification system was installed in the nave. A number of speakers in octagonal boxes, each about 15 inches high and approximately 12 inches in diameter were suspended from the vaulting to hang above the heads of the congregation, about 15 feet above the floor. In addition to interfering with the sight lines for the congregation, these speakers were unsightly and they were not exceptionally effective by today's standards. Architect Philip Frohman thought this was an inappropriate location for sound amplification. As he told Feller, "If all sound were to come from above our heads, the Lord would have turned our ears up rather than forward."

A few years after Feller arrived at the cathedral, Richard Wayne Dirksen, the Assistant Choir Master, was instructed by Dean Sayre to obtain and install the most effective sound system available, provided that the Clerk of the Works approved the aesthetics of the system. Fortunately, by that time rather more sophisticated systems had become available.

The system installed provides for speakers mounted vertically on several of the principal piers at the crossing. The speakers are covered by a light gray screen cloth that causes the installation to blend into the color of the stone piers. Each of the installations holds a number of speakers directed to different parts of the cathedral to assure that sound is transmitted effectively to the total nave.

After the speaker columns were installed, Feller had a set of iron brackets placed under each series of speakers so that they would appear to be supporting the speakers. The brackets are installed for visual effect only.

Still there were complaints from people about sound levels during services. There appeared to be pockets or areas of the nave where the level of sound varied, even during the service. Although the cathedral possessed a state-of-the-art public address system, it became obvious that a sound engineer was needed who could manually control and balance the system. As a result, a wooden platform approximately eight feet in diameter was constructed and placed midway toward the rear of the nave. This hexagon platform contains controls that allow the engineer to make changes in the direction and volume of sound to all areas of the nave. It is a very complex piece of equipment that is connected by an umbilical cord through the floor to all of the microphones and speakers in the cathedral.

To Give, *but not to Count the Cost*

In the final analysis, the story of building a cathedral is a story of people rather than building materials or processes. It becomes a story of those who plan the facility, those who construct the fabric and those who give the means that make it all possible. Mrs. Olive King was one of the latter.

Mrs. King and her husband had owned property on the Eastern Shore of Maryland that became a large housing development and that brought them a substantial sum of money. Unable to have children, she and her husband adopted four orphans. Typical of this gracious lady, she gave them a home with much love and affection.

She became interested in the cathedral and wanted to contribute to its construction. Because stained-glass artist Rowan LeCompte had grown up on the Eastern Shore of Maryland, she was especially enamored of his work.

There are five large windows high in the apse of the cathedral that reflect the life of Christ:

✦ The Childhood of Jesus (north side)
✦ The Crucifixion (east wall)
✦ Christ in Majesty (center of east wall)
✦ The Resurrection (east wall)
✦ The Transfiguration. (south side)

There was no difficulty in obtaining donors for the middle three windows since they would always be highly visible from the nave as well as from the Great Choir. The first and fifth windows, however, on the north and south sides of the chancel, could be seen only by someone standing in the chancel. They would not be visible to anyone seated in the nave and only limited sightlines would be available to anyone seated in the eastern end of the Great Choir.

In her modesty, Mrs. King was pleased to provide the funds for these two windows. She asked only that consideration be given to having Rowan LeCompte receive the commission for them. Her delight was in what she was able to do, not in the recognition she might receive for doing it. At a later date, she also gave the funds for two of the mosaics in the Resurrection Chapel, completed by Rowan and his late wife Irene.

Olive King, a person of deep commitment, unlimited generosity and true humility must be included in any list as one of the true builders of the Washington National Cathedral.

The Gift of the Garth Fountain

Several duPont sisters of Wilmington, Delaware, graduates of the National Cathedral School for Girls, asked to make a gift of a sculpture to the cathedral in memory of their parents. Specifically, they wanted the cathedral to select a conservative subject, probably a statue of a saint to be erected somewhere on the cathedral close. The Dean and Building Committee selected the garth, the enclosure between the north transept, the choir and the two cloisters leading to the Administration Building, as an appropriate site for this memorial. It was further proposed by the Dean that the sculpture should be an abstract work of art, preferably a fountain. Dean Sayre believed that all figure statues should be kept in the fabric of the cathedral.

The artists selected to submit competitive designs asked the Clerk of the Works repeatedly what kind of design was wanted. Feller told them that the Building Committee would know what they wanted when they saw it.

In due time, 11 designs from six different artists were presented to the Building Committee for their consideration, each of which was rejected. Finally, an appropriate design was received from artist George Tsutakawa, of Seattle, Washington. It was then necessary to take the design to the donors to be sure they were satisfied with it as their memorial. Normally, the Dean would have gone to visit the donors and secured their agreement to sponsor this work of art, but he was in Asia on a six month sabbatical. It was Feller's responsibility, therefore, to get the family's agreement so the cathedral could proceed with the project. He received a luncheon invitation from one of the sisters to come to her home and present the project for consideration. The artist had submitted a delightful little maquette, about 15 inches high, which Feller took along with slides of the artist's previous work.

The Garth Fountain.
Designed by Geroge Tsutakawa.

Photo by Stewart Brothers

Feller found this to be a most uncomfortable experience He was ushered into a room where there were nine women, duPont sisters and their daughters, but no other men. Feller felt the sense of intimidation with which many men are familiar, being surrounded by women with no male support. Instead of the work of art, he felt he was on display.

After lunch, the group adjourned to a large drawing room where a projector was set up and he showed slides of how the Building Committee anticipated the garth would look when the project was completed. Feller had known this would be a difficult experience since they all wanted and expected a very conservative presentation of a saint's statue, not the rather avant garde abstract fountain they were about to see. There were many questions and much discussion about the project but finally he asked them to consider the proposal and let the cathedral know their decision.

About two days after his visit, Feller received a call from one of the sisters saying that there was some disagreement among them but that they had voted and a majority had favored the project as presented.

When Dean Sayre returned from Asia, Feller told him of the approval and the Dean was delighted. He said that Feller must be quite a salesman and quipped that duPonts, along with the Cabots and Lodges in Massachusetts, only speak with God and Bishops.

This garth fountain raises an interesting observation. The spirit and feeling of the fountain is totally Japanese. The artist, George Tsutakawa, born in America, received his early education in Japan returning to this country for his adult life. But the garth does unite the orient with an English Gothic cathedral and the marriage is most compatible.

After the fountain was completed and dedicated, Dean Sayre gave Feller the small maquette of the garth fountain for his personal collection of cathedral souvenirs. However, Feller has since returned the maquette to the collection of cathedral artifacts.

The Explosive Master Carver

Roger Morigi, appointed Master Carver at the cathedral in the 1950s, was one of the finest stone carvers the cathedral had been privileged to employ. Not only did he do fine stone carving but he also trained younger carvers who made outstanding contributions to the cathedral. Morigi had two other attributes that were well known to his colleagues, a keen sense of humor and a most explosive temper.

John Guarenti, in addition to being a very good stone carver was essentially a nomad. He worked at the cathedral a number of months each year and then wanted to be off and away. His hobby was repairing old flintlock rifles and then using them for hunting. As one might suspect, he was something of a "loner" and consequently did not take orders too willingly, especially from the Master Carver, his fellow Italian Morigi.

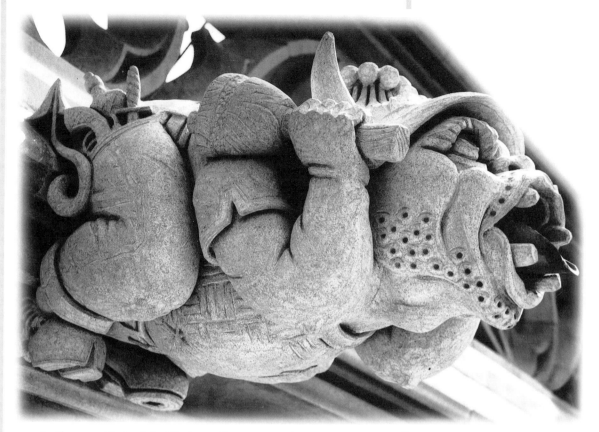

As the new Clerk of the Works, Feller oversaw the progress of the stone carvers. At the time there were about nine carvers working on various assignments in the nave and working at separate locations, but Guarenti was a sufficiently talented stone carver that he was allowed to fashion his own gargoyles. On one occasion, Feller climbed the scaffold to look at Guarenti's work and looking at his stone he asked, "John, what on earth are you making?"

Guarenti responded that it was just "sort of a head" that would become a gargoyle. Feller was suspicious because he noted the top of the head appeared to be erupting in an atomic explosion. On one side a pocket held golf clubs while on the other side, the pocket contained chisels and mallets of the carver's trade as well as a pistol and stiletto. Everything emerging from the stone made Feller think of Morigi, the Master Carver.

"Are you doing a caricature of Morigi?" Feller inquired.

"Oh no," John replied, "I like my job here."

Of course it did turn out to be precisely what Feller thought it was and it is now one of the most memorable and best known of all the gargoyles at the cathedral. Morigi has probably enjoyed the gargoyle more than anyone although he insisted that it was not a very good likeness.

Gargoyle caricature of Roger Morigi. Carved by John Guarenti.

Photo by Stewart Brothers

The Te Deum Windows

The apse of the cathedral was designed entirely by George Bodley and Henry Vaughn, the first two architects of Washington National Cathedral. Philip Frohman had very little to do with the apse although he

57

did on several occasions attempt to correct a pre-existing condition.

At the clerestory level, there are five windows with themes on the life of Christ. Two of these windows were designed and installed in later years. Further to the west, but adjoining these five windows, are the *Te Deum* windows, one on each side of the chancel. Each window consists of six lancets installed in three banks of two lancets each. Extending downward from the vaulting to approximately eight feet above the floor, these openings were installed to admit light to the chancel during daytime services.

The glass in these windows has not been successful. Covered with a black paint matting to age them, the windows are also crowded with figures. They are generally dark and they should some day be replaced.

When Frohman, Robb and Little were appointed architects of the cathedral in 1921, Philip Frohman was a young man and some members of the Building Committee questioned whether he had sufficient experience to handle Gothic design. At the time, Dr. Ralph Adams Cram, who was a well known lecturer and writer on Gothic architecture, and who was also a principal architect for the Cathedral of St. John the Divine in New York, had been retained as a consultant to meet with the Building Committee on occasion and to advise concerning the Frohman firm's designs. As one might imagine, this created the perfect environment for conflict and the two appeared a number of times before the Building Committee to defend opposing points of view. More frequently than not, Mr. Frohman's point was accepted by the Building Committee. This created some ill feeling and led Frohman to question whether Dr. Cram was competent to advise on Gothic architectural matters.

Frohman felt his suspicions were confirmed when on one occasion Dr. Cram advised the Building Committee that more windows should be in the sanctuary to admit light to the area. In the ensuing debate, it became apparent that Cram had never noticed the *Te Deum* windows and was unaware of their presence.

The Ambry door in the chancel. Designed and fabricated by Herbert Read, St. Sidwell's Art Studio, Exeter, England.

The Ambry Door

In the chancel, on the eastern side of a pier in the north wall, seen only by a priest at the High Altar, is the ambry where reserved sacraments may be kept between eucharistic services. By 1960, a proper door had never been created for this ambry and it had been covered for decades by a piece of rough plywood.

During one of his early trips to England on cathedral business, Feller planned to visit the St. Sidwell's Art Studios in Exeter. Dean Sayre suggested that while he was there, he might inquire about the cost of a suitable door for the ambry. Feller met with Herbert Read at the Exeter studio, explained the need for an ambry door and gave him the dimensions. When Read asked where the ambry was located, Feller replied that it was in the old part of the cathedral.

Read then asked how old the old part of the cathedral was and it was at that moment that Feller realized his foot was firmly in his mouth. He admitted to Read, an English business man accustomed to working with English cathedrals six to seven centuries old, that the older part of the Washington Cathedral was only about 30-years-old. Mr. Read replied that he found that very interesting.

Feller has considered Read to have been a true gentleman since he had such a perfect opportunity to laugh but refrained from doing so. Sometimes, the kindest memories are not for the things we do, but the things we don't do.

Sculpting the Majestus

Very early the Building Committee understood that the Majestus in the center of the High Altar reredos would probably be the most important piece of sculpture in the entire cathedral. Not only was it necessary that this project be treated with great sensitivity, but it was thought inappropriate that it be given as a memorial to any individual. All costs associated with the Majestus, therefore, were covered from the endowment income of the cathedral and not from any special gift.

The space allowed by the architect in the center of the reredos for the Majestus figure was not large enough to accommodate a standing figure. With a seated figure, however, the prominence of the knees proved to be a problem that artists could not solve. Several artists submitted proposals but none was accepted by the Building Committee. As a temporary expedient, a plaster model that had been submitted for consideration was left in place for more than thirty years just to fill the space in the reredos. To the average visitor it gave the appearance of stone.

There were several problems that an artist needed to deal with in addition to the limited space in the reredos for the sculpture. The greatest challenge was the sight lines. The sculpture had to be seen clearly at close range by persons at the communion rail and by those entering the west end of the cathedral, a distance of one tenth of a mile. Secondly, the sculpture needed to show the seated Christ extending a blessing with his right hand while holding a globe symbolizing the world in his left hand.

After a 30-year hiatus, Dean Sayre decided to confront the problem again. Walker Hancock, a distinguished American sculptor, was selected and commissioned to create a new model. He was successful and the Building Committee approved his submission. Master Carver Roger Morigi then completed the carving.

When the initial work had been accomplished on the reredos in the 1920s, the stone selected came from quarries at Caen in Normandy. This particular stone had been selected by Frohman because of the light cream color which gave a feeling of warmth. Additional blocks of stone for the Majestus had also been purchased and stored in large boxes in the construction yard where it remained for many, many years. Finally, when the model by Hancock was approved, the boxes were opened to disclose stone that had become so very soft it would not hold an edge and therefore could not be carved.

Because the quarries of Caen had been worked out and abandoned, a search began for a substitute stone. The goal was to find a stone that was near enough in color that it could be used with the Caen stone in the reredos. After a world-wide search, a limestone in Texas was selected and used. Three separate stone pieces were needed, each weighing approximately five tons.

When the Majestus was installed, there were two more problems to address. First, the Majestus figure appeared too light in color when compared with the color of the Caen stone in the reredos background. This mismatch was overcome by Carl Tucker, a member of the cathedral staff, but that is another story that is told elsewhere. The second problem was providing the right light, properly focused on the sculpture. Hancock wanted the light used on the sculpture to allow the appropriate shadows and enhancements so that the details of the sculpture would be seen properly. Lighting consultants spent a considerable time experimenting until the proper solution was achieved.

Let There Be Light

Over his years of work on the cathedral, Richard Feller felt his education was enlarged considerably both by Philip Hubert Frohman and by Walker Hancock. He learned the importance of proper sight lines and the way they may be enhanced by the use of lighting to achieve a better view of the details of both construction and sculpture.

In Gothic architecture especially, the employment of moldings and ledges can serve to break the plane of a building surface and to introduce a greater beauty and interest by the way that light plays on these changes in elevation. The use of light properly directed in the interior of the building can emphasize architectural features that otherwise might be missed. For this reason, the use of lights to increase the brightness in the building may be secondary to the way the lights play on the surfaces in the building.

When the central tower was under construction, Frohman was inspecting the stone work on the tower and remarked to Feller that he regretted not making a molding near the top of the tower larger by one-eighth of an inch. When Feller commented that the molding, 25 stories above the ground could not be seen by anyone from the surface, Frohman responded that the shadow it created would have been so much more pronounced and would have enhanced the tower's appearance.

In the same respect, Hancock was concerned with the play of artificial light on a sculpture. He emphasized that a great piece of sculpture could be shown at a real disadvantage if the light directed toward it showed the wrong shadows. He spent a considerable amount of time at the cathedral to consult on lighting for both his sculpture of the Majestus in the reredos, and the figure of President Lincoln at the rear of the nave. In the first instance, lighting consultants experimented with lights located at many different places, directing lights toward the Majestus from different angles before the desired effect was achieved.

In the second instance, the base on which the Lincoln statue rests was adjusted in height, moved several times, and turned in order to achieve the proper illumination. These are small but important details that are seldom noted by the thousands of tourists who visit the cathedral.

Transfer of the Angels

As the cathedral was rising, one of the great challenges for Dean Sayre was to develop the iconography, the use of symbols, sculptures, stained glass and tapestries to tell the stories of the Bible. By tradition, Old Testament characters, the prophets, kings and writers are always shown on the north side of a cathedral while those associated with the New Testament are displayed on the south side. The reason for this differentiation is to allow the brighter illumination that comes fom the southern exposure of the building to represent the greater light that came to the world from the advent of the Son of God.

During the 1950s when Dean Sayre and Richard Feller were discussing the iconography of the cathedral, they determined to continue the original concept developed early in the life of the cathedral, namely that the clerestory windows of the Great Choir would all represent angels of the Biblical stories. To their consternation, they discovered that three of the earliest windows installed on the north side were angels of the New Testament that should have been installed on the south side. This matter concerned the two of them for several years knowing that it would be a major undertaking to move the windows. Even though the average visitor would be unaware of the differences, they believed that the windows should be moved in order that the iconography be correct.

The original windows were designed and fabricated by the artist Lawrence Saint at his studio near Philadelphia. Since Mr. Saint had long since died, the contract to move the windows was given to stained-glass artist Rowan LeCompte and his fabricator Dieter Goldkuhle, both of whom were working at the cathedral on other windows.

The Saint windows had been in place for a long period of time by then and the putty used to install them had hardened and become brittle so that it was not possible to remove the windows without destroying the borders around them. It was necessary then for LeCompte to replace the borders. In the first window, the border was replaced almost precisely as it had been in the original Saint window. In the second window, however, LeCompte being the perfectionist that he is, made some changes in the border that resulted in an improved window. In the third window, however, he agreed not to make changes in the original Saint window.

LeCompte was commissioned to design and install the remainder of the clerestory windows in the Great Choir. This represented the first clerestory windows commissioned to LeCompte who since has been commissioned to complete all of the remaining nave clerestory windows in the cathedral, a life-long task for the artist.

Pigeons, Pigeons, Pigeons

In any construction in the Northern Hemisphere, one is almost certain to be visited, if not harrassed, by pigeons. Over the years, they contributed greatly to the vexations associated with building the cathedral since it was also necessary to maintain portions of the building in readiness at all times for religious services. Some control could be exercised by attempting to block off all openings but when a new window was installed, a new addition built or the nave extended by an additional bay, pigeons were almost certain to make their way inside.

Finally, someone discovered that the birds did not fly into the cathedral. They would land on portions of the scaffolding and walk in. But once when they were inside, they were unable to find their way back outside.

During the late 1960s, a visiting Italian choral group was to sing in concert. A pair of pigeons had found their way into the building and were, in fact, nesting right over the place where the conductor would stand. Organist and choirmaster Dirksen told the conductor about this in explaining why he wanted to move the conductor's podium. The conductor was delighted. In Italy, he explained, the presence of pigeons would be a most fortuitous happening since it foretold that the concert would be successful. It was.

On several occasions, pigeons would get into the cathedral on a Saturday and on Sunday morning they would fly back and forth from one transept to another, distracting the congregation from the sermon. The pigeons nearly upstaged the clergy, as well as the Secret Service, at the funeral for President Eisenhower. Of course the funeral service was televised by all of the major networks. There were trailers full of television equipment outside the cathedral and technicians were crawling around inside the building trying to connect their cameras to the trailers by cables running between the two areas. At the same time, since there would be many government officials, visiting heads of state as well as members of the diplomatic corps in attendance, the Secret Service was sweeping the building with their usual diligence. In the midst of these preparations, two pigeons were discovered flying around in the cathedral. They must be removed, especially since President DeGaulle of France would be in attendance and it had been reported that he had a special phobia about pigeons. Whenever any problem arose at the cathedral that was in the least degree unusual in nature, it was referred to the Clerk of the Works. Accordingly, Richard Feller was called.

Initially, Feller wanted to determine how the pigeons got into the building in the first place. In this instance, a technician had opened a window at an upper level for cables to be brought in and had failed to close it. The pigeons had walked in as if they had been invited. Feller had a piece of plywood cut to fit the opening so that it could be secured and additional pigeons could not get in.

Secondly, it was necessary to get rid of the two pigeons in the building. In the cathedral's vast interior space, only one method had been found effective; a sharp shooter with a small rifle was able to bring them down. It was used, the pigeons were dispatched, the networks obtained their pictures and the funeral service took place as planned.

Baptismal Font

One of the earliest construction projects on Mt. St. Alban, was the construction of a Baptistry, a total immersion baptismal font. In later years this concept was abandoned, and the building intended to be the Baptistry became instead the Herb Cottage. At that point, it was decided to install a more traditional font in the cathedral.

An ornate baptismal font of Tennessee pink marble was installed in the west aisle of the cathedral's south transept. It was equipped with piping so that it might be filled with water and also drained, making it unnecessary to carry water to or from the font.

There is a handsome wooden cover for the font that was designed and completed by the St. Sidwell's Art Studios in Exeter, England. This was the first piece of wood sculpture supplied by St. Sidwell's for the Washington National Cathedral. It has been followed by many more pieces of wood sculpture during four decades.

Interestingly enough, this large font is almost never used. Since the large majority of all baptisms in the Episcopal Communion are for children or infants, the baptism services are held in the Children's Chapel, the Chapel of the Resurrection or in Bethlehem Chapel where there are smaller fonts available.

Baptisimal font in the south transept. Cover designed by the St. Sidwell's Art Studio, Exeter, England.

Dean Sayre's Woodworking Hobby

Dean Sayre had his own home woodworking shop that provided the locus for his principal hobby. He was quite a craftsman, able to make furniture for his children. His art training also helped him to do simple wood carving.

When the wall panel boxes providing electrical distribution to areas of the cathedral were installed, there was no money for decorative covers for them, just the plain metal covers that are typically used in an industrial setting. These were hardly the kind of surfaces one would want exposed in a Gothic cathedral, so the Dean created more fitting sculptured wooden covers for the panels that were visible in the cathedral. There are three panel box covers made by Dean Sayre, all located in the north transept.

There is a fourth cover that demonstrates the Dean's sense of humor. It is in a small room to the rear of St. John's Chapel. The door is covered with Gothic tracery and behind it all is the head of a priest with his hand extended, seeming to say, "Hey, let me out of here!"

Fortunately, the little priest has never been rescued. He continues to call from his prison of tracery.

Electrical distribution panel cover designed and carved by Dean Sayre.

Conservation of the Rood Beam

In the winter of 1989, when it was not possible to do construction work on the exterior of the cathedral, scaffolding was erected in the nave so that masons could examine the vaulting and determine if any preventive maintenance could be performed. Specifically, they removed any cracked or broken pieces of stone or of mortar that might fall. In addition, any courses where mortar was missing were filled either with new mortar or with caulking.

While the scaffolding was in place, the rood beam that had been in place for about 60 years was inspected to be sure that it was still sturdy and stable. Much to the relief of Feller, it was discovered that the rood beam was not composed of wood only but that it also encased a steel beam firmly fixed to the piers on each side of the Great Choir. The wooden crucifixion sculpture was leaning slightly, however, so that a steel cable invisible from the floor was affixed to the sculpture and thence to the vaulting above to ensure the sculpture would never fall.

As the wood was slightly dry, it was cleaned and then treated with linseed oil to preserve it. Finally, a brief note was sealed in an envelope and stapled to the top of the beam, that would inform future generations what had been done to the rood beam to preserve it. The note included the names of the cathedral construction crew. Thus, the members of the crew have now had their names inscribed in high places, far above their expectations.

Completing the West Towers

In the early stages of construction projects, plans tend to be more grandiose than the constraints of future budgets allow. In the initial planning for the two west towers, it had been envisioned that an elevator would be installed in each tower that could carry people from the observation gallery, seventh floor level, to the top of the tower, with intermediate floors installed to be used as office space. In the early 1980s, when it was decided that we could indeed resume construction on the two towers and carry them through to completion, something had to be sacrificed.

The installation of two passenger elevators would have required approximately $750,000 each—more money than was available. The elevators were deferred as well as the completion of the intervening floors in the two towers. Each of the towers has been constructed with cross beams, that could be used in the future for the installation of floors, but in the interim they serve to reinforce the towers against wind forces at that level. The cross beams are installed in such a manner that they provide the maximum in strength for the towers but also will accommodate elevators for some future generation.

The Auditorium

Although the Washington Cathedral is built in the manner of a pure Gothic structure such as those of England and France, we still have been able to include a number of innovations because of the modern construction technology available today. Following the pattern of building a floor over the vaulting of the south transept, a floor was built over the nave vaulting creating an overcroft for the cathedral. Here was an opportunity to create additional good, usable space that could function effectively for the cathedral.

As the construction of the west end continued, the decision was made to build an auditorium in the overcroft of the nave. There was some misgiving among the safety inspectors of the District of Columbia but since each tower was constructed with both an elevator as well as dual staircases, it was agreed that an auditorium of not more than 199 seats could be installed. The Perry Auditorium, named for Provost Charles Perry, that opens off the Pilgrim Gallery at the seventh floor level, provides a facility that enables the cathedral to offer an expanded program for visitors.

In addition to a projection booth at the rear of the auditorium that allows films to be shown, there is also an area beyond the auditorium that can accommodate TV production facilities. This room now lacks the modern technological equipment that will one day enable it to serve as a television studio.

The Lincoln Statue

At the west end of each nave outer aisle, the architect designed very stately and high vaulted bays intended to contain monumental sculpture. The south bay, adjoining the Rare Book Library, is the Washington Bay. It contains the Vermont white marble statue of President George Washington that was created by artist Lee Lawrie. A native of Germany, he instructed in sculpture at both Yale and Harvard.

The corresponding bay in the north aisle is the Lincoln Bay. In many respects, the two bays were to be the antithesis of each other. The south bay was to symbolize the optimism in the new life of the nation while the north bay would represent the upheaval, the breach in the nation's life brought about by the Civil War. The medium for the Washington sculpture was white marble; for Lincoln it was to be bronze. The stained glass in the south bay is light, full of hope. In the north bay, the glass symbolizes the torment, the bloodshed and the tearing of the nation's fabric.

Because he was such a central figure in our national history, there are probably more sculptures of Lincoln in the country than of any other American. And it would be difficult for any artist to execute an acceptable work in the same city where Daniel Chester French's masterful seated Lincoln is on display in the Lincoln Memorial. Still there had to be something special, in fact unique, about a statue of Lincoln at the cathedral.

Walker Hancock, one of the more outstanding sculptors in the country, was between commissions and agreed to consider the project. Lincoln's farewell remarks to his friends and neighbors in Springfield when he left for Washington was to be carved into the wall that would be behind the statue. These words, then, provided not only the background for the sculpture but set the mood for the statue as well. When it was finally finished and installed, the statue became the last item in the Lincoln Bay to be completed, yet it is the central item of interest.

Embarrassing Moments

There are always those moments in the interplay of a group of persons when words are uttered or actions taken that obviously have not been preceded by an adequate amount of thought. Such instances have occurred among cathedral employees and volunteers as well; instances that although embarrassing at the moment, subsequently serve to lighten what might otherwise be more unrewarding moments.

✚ When he picked up his check at the payroll office, one of the cathedral administrators was told by the clerk, "You make so much money that it causes the machine to stutter."

✚ Canon John Walker, the first African-American Canon at the cathedral, was asked for identification by the payroll clerk who told him, "All of you canons look alike to me."

✚ Some artists tend to be less than humble about their talents, even though they have every reason to be. Canon Feller remembers one sculptor, who was more impressed with his ability in producing a small 30-inch sculpture for the cathedral than he was of the building in which it was to be placed. The man wore a Phi Beta Kappa key and just barely resisted the temptation to surround it with neon lights.

The artist came to the cathedral to see his statue that had been installed, arriving during the annual Flower Mart that is held each year in May. The cathedral and the close were filled with thousands of people enjoying the mart. The artist convinced himself, however, that everyone was there to see his artistic endeavor only. Feller bit his lip to keep from laughing, and showed great restraint in doing nothing to disavow the artist's conviction.

✚ During a memorial service after the death of Winston Churchill, an Army Colonel in full dress uniform, attempting to maintain the decorum that such an occasion demanded, tripped over his ceremonial sword in the processional and fell flat.

✚ When the Rare Book Library was first opened, a security system was installed that included electric eyes intended to trip an elaborate alarm system when any motion was detected. One of the cathedral cleaners repeatedly created havoc by insisting on dusting the electric eyes.

✚ One of the things that distresses docents at the cathedral is the misinformation given touring groups by outside tour guides. As an example, in St. John's Chapel is the tomb of Lt. Norman Prince, the founder of the Lafayette Escadrille during World War I. A guide was overheard telling her group about the tomb and then adding, "You have all heard about Snoopy and the Red Baron. This is the tomb of the Red Baron."

✚ It is generally known that George Washington was an active member of the Masons, and, in fact served as the Grand Master of his Lodge during his later years. In order to commemorate this fact, a group of Masons in the District of Columbia gave the funds to create the marble sculpture of our first President. When the sculpture was completed in 1967, it was set up temporarily in the north transept of the cathedral and a group of Masons was invited to the dedication ceremony. Unfortunately, it was a group of Masons who had contributed nothing to the sculpture. This was a most regrettable mistake.

In 1976, when the nave was completed, the sculpture was moved from the north transept to its present location in the southwest corner of the nave. On this occasion, a new dedication ceremony was held and the correct and proper Masonic group was invited to attend.

Marble statue of
President George Washington
by sculptor Lee Lawrie.

Cathedral Archives

✝ When the George M. Fuller Company serving as the general contractor was constructing the main portion of the nave, a time keeper who appeared to be quite harried with his responsibilities asked the building superintendent, "Does Easter fall on Sunday this year?"

✝ Because of the friendliness he exhibited typically to all people, Dean Sayre had been made an honorary member of the Bricklayer's Union. He was talking with a new member of the administrative staff one day and mentioned in passing that he was a member of the union. In all seriousness she asked, "Now that the union is on strike, are you required to walk the picket line?"

✝ For many years, Dean Sayre and General Thomas White, Chief of Staff of the Air Force, had been close friends. When the General died, a funeral was to be held at the cathedral with Dean Sayre officiating. A day or so before the funeral, the Dean saw two junior Air Force Officers in the parking lot adjoining the cathedral counting the parking spaces available and he asked what they were doing. Impressed with the seriousness of the occasion and the importance of their responsibilities, they told him they were on a "classified assignment."

✝ Richard Feller was amused to receive a package from Railway Express addressed to "Clerk of the Monks."

✝ Mr. Frohman was a man with a keen sense of dry humor. He remarked to Feller one day that he hoped his design for the Gloria in Excelcis Tower would be so elevating that it would be unnecessary to install an elevator in the tower.

✝ Donors to the cathedral come in all shapes and sizes. One donor who was well known to all at the cathedral was a little lady, a widow, who had a very noticeable limp and who was required to sit and rest frequently. She was a modest person who always dressed in an unassuming manner; she wore a small red hat with a feather. On one occasion, Dean Sayre was escorting a group of cathedral deans from Canada through the building when one of his visitors commented, "Well, I am certain that you must have some very imposing donors, members of the upper class in your country who give you very generous gifts for the construction of the cathedral." Dean Sayre replied, "Not all of the persons who give are members of what you would consider to be the aristocracy. That little woman sitting over there with the red hat has just given us a million dollars."

Richard Wayne Dirksen

Photo by Morton Broffman

He was certain to become a musician. His mother was a singer and the church organist, his father a builder of organs and the founder of The Freeport Organ Company of Illinois. His early musical training was with fine local teachers of piano and organ, augmented with six years of instrumental experience as a bassoonist, drummer, and student conductor in the excellent public schools music programs of Illinois.

Having completed all of his musical goals in Freeport High School, Dirksen studied privately for two years with Dr. Hugh Price, a faculty member of the American Conservatory in Chicago. He studied advanced piano and organ as well as harmony, theory, and counterpoint with the goal of earning a major scholarship. He did. He went to the Peabody Conservatory in Baltimore in 1940 on a full scholarship where he studied under the young but already world famous concert artist, Virgil Fox. In June 1942, having completed a three year program in two years, he played his senior recital, won an award and was graduated with honors and a Church Organist Certificate. His next move was to enlist in the United States Army.

For four months before his enlistment in 1942, Dirksen had commuted several times a week from Baltimore to Washington, serving as a part-time assistant to Paul Callaway who was at that time the Organist and Choirmaster at Washington National Cathedral. After his discharge from the Army in late 1945, Dirksen was asked to help the interim organist over the Christmas season. When Callaway returned from his assignment as an Army bandmaster in the spring of 1946, Dirksen worked at the cathedral as an associate of Callaway's until the latter's retirement in 1977 at which time Dirksen was appointed the cathedral's fourth Organist and Choirmaster. Later he was named Canon Precentor, in charge of all services, the first lay person to hold this post.

In April of 1991 Dirksen retired as Canon Precentor, Emeritus, after 49 years with the cathedral. In 1994 he published an annotated catalog of the more than 350 compositions he created for the cathedral, its schools, and for churches and musicians across the country. In retirement he still composed on occasion, joining with his wife Joan who had also contributed as a librettist. He has a happy and full memory of his many years at Washington National Cathedral and he enjoys recalling them, punctuating his recollections with a most infectious and hearty laugh.

The stories that follow are a part of that recollection. They are all happy stories. Listen to them.

Water, Water Everywhere

When Dirksen first came to Washington National Cathedral as an assistant to Paul Callaway, the cloister where the choir rehearsed was little more than a two-story Gothic stub that extended northward from St. Mary's Chapel sacristy on the second level and from the Bethlehem Chapel north crypt aisle on the lower level. Along that crypt aisle towards the parclose stairs was the men's restroom; the only source of water on that level on the north side of the cathedral. It was in 1954 that someone suggested a bottled water fountain could be installed in the choir room. The glass bottle held five gallons and it had to be filled in the restroom, 60 yards away. With only two verger-sexton-cleaners on the cathedral's staff, it obviously fell to Dirksen to tend the bottle. Not only did he need to traverse the 60 yards to fill the bottle, he had to go up and down stairs and open heavy oak doors; and with each step the bottle became heavier.

It was also Dirksen's responsibility to rehearse the junior boy's choir. Having completed his education at the Peabody Conservatory, having served through three years of World War II, and being both a husband and parent, Dirksen was a serious young man in the early 1950s and he expected that the 24 young boys in the choir would be serious musicians. They chose instead, to contribute further to *his* education.

Dirksen was concerned that water not be wasted but conserved and used wisely. Nevertheless, the choir boys were delighted with the availability of the water and the paper cup holder that was mounted near to the fountain. In fact, they were so delighted with this new addition to the choir room, that when Dirksen was absent, they engaged in a contest to see how much water they could douse on each other.

When Dirksen returned, he explained patiently the difficulty the staff experienced in trying to keep things neat and orderly as well as the difficulty one experienced in filling the water jug. Never, never, never were they to engage in water fights again nor to waste that precious water. The choir boys were to be models of decorum. All of the boys understood this and would comply. There would be no further water fights. Would there?

Of course there were.

Dirksen ordered the entire junior choir back on a Saturday morning. At 9:00 A.M. they took their place around the piano and watched as Dirksen emptied the five gallon jug out of the window. He then explained how the jug was to be filled. The boys would be given two of the two-ounce paper cups, one for each hand, and they would proceed 60 yards to the restroom, fill their cups with water, retrace their steps to the choir room and pour the water in the narrow neck of the jug. They were cautioned against haste that would result in spilling the water and therefore delay the exercise.

The choirmaster had planned the exercise as meticulously as a general laying out a military campaign.

✚ Every ten seconds, four ounces of water added to the jug.

✚ Every five minutes and 20 seconds a gallon of water in the jug.

✚ In 26 minutes, 40 seconds the exercise would be ended.

But exercises have a way of failing to fulfill the plans that are made for them. After an hour the jug was still only half full. Dirksen realized that he was experiencing the great Chinese water torture, not the boys. Like the good military strategist, he cut his losses, called a halt to the exercise, had the boys mop the floor with paper towels and then participate in a debriefing.

It worked. Water fights never held any fascination for the boy's choir again, not when they had to work so hard in order to play.

Standing Tall in the Choir Stalls

In the late 1940s and early 1950s, the Junior Boys Choir sang only in Bethlehem Chapel on Sunday mornings and St. Joseph of Arimathea Chapel for Evensong during the week. At the conclusion of their seven months of training, on Palm Sunday morning, they would finally get to go upstairs into the stalls of the Great Choir and sing the nine o'clock service. They were excited about this opportunity and they anticipated the occasion with enthusiasm. The final rehearsal was scheduled for the Friday afternoon before Palm Sunday.

The boys knew their music by heart. The only requirement was to have them practice the processional, sit in the choir stalls, and then sing the music through with the Great Organ, still a vastly dif-

Junior choir boys in procession.

Cathedral Archives

ferent experience for them. From the organ console, Choirmaster Dirksen signaled for the choir to stand and to prepare to sing their anthem. He looked in the reflecting mirror to check their response and their posture, but they were not standing. He gave the signal again and still no heads or shoulders appeared.

This was more than the Choirmaster was prepared to accept. He stood and shouted to the Junior Boys to, "Stand up!" It was then that he saw 20 little heads jumping up and down to show him they were standing. They were just not as tall as the stalls. Dirksen was more accustomed to seeing the Senior Boys in the Great Choir who averaged about ten inches taller.

The little fellows laughed; when they saw that the Choirmaster was also convulsed with laughter, they laughed as much from relief as from amusement.

Canon Luther D. Miller, Sr.

Canon Luther D. Miller, Sr. was a different kind of canon at the cathedral. Unlike most of the clergy who are appointed canons, he had already retired once. He had served a full career in the United States Army as a Chaplain and at the conclusion of that career, he was Chief of Chaplains for the Army. Not only that, but he had attained the rank of Major General.

Born in 1890, Luther Miller, Sr. attended Chicago Theological Seminary graduating in 1917. He was ordained a priest and after being inducted into the United States Army, completed Chaplain School in 1922. He served continuously until his retirement in 1945.

Canon Miller almost always sang Evensong during the week. Wayne Dirksen marveled at the man. He would stand at the exit to the chapel and greet everyone leaving. His personality was such that people felt obligated to speak with him and it was only on rare occasions that he did not encounter someone he either knew or who knew a mutual acquaintance. And this could happen if only two or three were in attendance. Dirksen still believes that Canon Miller must either have baptised, performed a wedding ceremony or held confirmation classes for most of the United States Army.

The Battle of the Pipes

The annual service for the St. Andrews Society, the "Kirkin' o' the Tartan", was always held on a Sunday morning in May. Several hundred Scotsmen, dressed in their clan colors and full formal regalia, were always led into the Great Choir by a large bagpipe band, the St. Andrews Pipers and Drummers. The plaids were carried before the High Altar and were blessed by the Dean. This colorful service filled the cathedral.

The great procession followed the offertory anthem and accompanied the presentation of the offerings at the altar. There was one occasion that will not soon be forgotten by anyone who was in attendance that day.

The offertory anthem on that occasion was *In the Year that King Uzziah Died*, by David McKay Williams. The music is fast and loud and exciting for about four minutes, but then quiets down to a very sustained and soft cadence. A brief silence ensues and then the music resumes fortissimo for a two-minute exciting close with the full organ. The band leader in the west end of the cathedral mistook the silent interlude to be the conclusion of the offertory music and his cue to begin the procession with the pipers and drummers. The three great booming beats of the bass drum set off the droning of the 30 bagpipes and they were off down the aisle.

Paul Callaway was the organist on this occasion and he was less than pleased with the interruption of his offertory. He threw on the full organ, and brought in the choir full force, in the attempt to have the organ pipes out-play the bagpipes. The band, meanwhile, getting closer to the great crossing seemed oblivious of the organ and the choir. They seemed to be holding their own. In desperation, Callaway brought in the great solo tuba pipes that were added to the whole mix.

The St. Andrews Pipes and Drummers, "Kirkin-o-the-Tartan."

Photo by David A. Werth

On this occasion, Dirksen was standing off to the side as page turner for Callaway. He was in a perfect position to determine who might blink first and which of the competitors would emerge victorious. There was even a question in his mind if the great crescendo of the many pipes might not bring some of the stained glass windows crashing down below.

Who won? Ever the diplomat, Dirksen declared it a draw. But he has very carefully avoided an opportunity to have a repeat encounter. This is one area in his mind, in which a "sudden death" competition might not be just a fanciful expression.

73

The Philanthropy of Miss Bessie J. Kibbey

In the late 1950s, Wayne Dirksen started planning for the bells that were to be installed in the central tower that was then under construction. Dirksen was told that some preliminary work had been done in previous years and so he went to the archives to see what he could find. It was at this point that he discovered the astounding contribution Miss Bessie J. Kibbey had made to the cathedral.

Miss Kibbey was a most generous benefactor of Washington Cathedral over a long period of time. In 1896, she was listed as the second person to make a gift to the new Diocese of Washington, sending the new Bishop Satterlee a gift of $15,000. Her gifts continued until her death in 1944. During this 48 years of philanthrophy, she made known her desire to give the bells for the great central tower in the cathedral. She had traveled abroad to visit bell foundries in Austria, Holland and England, and her thorough investigation had led to a conviction that the John Taylor & Sons Foundry at Loughborough, England would be the best choice to fill the order. It was her recommendation that a carillon of six octaves, a total of 73 bells should be cast and installed in the tower. She specified the bells on a chart provided by the Taylor Foundry, giving the weight of each bell, and even adding an inscription for each bell, choosing verses from her birthday psalms listed in the Book of Common Prayer lectionary.

Although Miss Kibbey had been most thorough in her selection of the bells for Washington National Cathedral, it was decided that some of them were not needed. As Dirksen explained it, the size of bells diminishes rapidly as the scales and octaves increase so that in the upper ranges the bells would be no larger than tea cups. Two hundred feet above grade, they could certainly not be heard at ground level. Only 53 bells for the carillon were installed. Over the years, the Kibbey gift had increased in value to the point that it not only covered the cost of the bells, it even provided some of the funds needed to construct the tower.

So today, because of the unique contributions made by Bessie J. Kibbey, contributions not only of money and of time, but a talent that she acquired and honed for many years, we are privileged to hear and enjoy the carillon that serves as her memorial.

The Trip to England

In March 1963, Wayne Dirksen, Richard Feller and Ronald Barnes, the cathedral's new carillonneur, all went as a group to the John Taylor Foundries in Loughborough, England to examine, test and accept the bells for the Cathedral Foundation. Asked about his recollection of that trip, the first thing that comes to Dirksen's mind is how cold it was.

The three of them drove from Heathrow Airport to Loughborough. Just north of Leicester and not far above Coventry, it was not a long trip but it seemed far longer. As Dirksen described it, "The overnight air journey and the difficulty of driving on the wrong side of the road all the way from London in a car that was built by someone with mirror vision, could only allow us to stagger out into the narrow street outside the foundry in a condition which certainly resembled advanced disease coupled with onsetting rigor mortis. Fortunately, for all of us, it was only a temporary condition."

Before they left Washington, the three had visited the central tower and had taken every last measurement down to a fraction of an inch to reassure themselves that adequate space was available for the carillon. In spite of this, when they saw the mounted framework in the foundry, with all of the bells, wires and clappers, Dirksen was convinced that the installation was far too big to fit in the tower. First impressions sometimes are faulty impressions.

During the following three days, the three visitors climbed to every part of the carillon and checked every connection, every bell, the large wooden keyboard, the levers and connecting wires, to be certain that everything worked as it was supposed to. If there were any faults in the installation, now was the time to discover them. After all of the bells had been shipped to Baltimore, transported to Washington, installed in the cathedral, it would be somewhat unseemly to find fault with them. Dirksen checked every bell for quality and intonation. He then tested them in every conceivable harmonic combination and he listened as Barnes played the carillon fast, slow, loud, soft. Two bells needed to be tuned very slightly and this was done quickly by the foundry.

On the last day, the delegation signed for the Cathedral Foundation, accepting the total installation. As they gathered in the office of the foundry to complete the paperwork, Dirksen looked at the thermometer on the office wall, and it indicated 54 degrees Fahrenheit. It's interesting that such a cool surrounding could evoke such warm memories.

The Bossanyi Window

It was on a subsequent trip Dirksen took to England in 1962, that he met Ervin Bossanyi, a stained-glass artist who lived in the small village of Eastcote near London. Dirksen recalls the visit with a sense of respect and tenderness for the artist. And Bossanyi deserved all of the accolades that we might tender him.

Some of the bells
in the Bessie J. Kibbey Carillon.

Born in Hungary, he later settled in Leipzig, Germany but fled from there to London in 1934. His early life was one of personal suffering and tragedy, and it greatly influenced his work in later years. He had lived through World War I and had experienced some of the terrors that preceded World War II. His greatest desire was to see people live together in peace.

Dirksen had been given a letter of introduction to the artist and he availed himself of the opportunity to visit. Bossanyi's home was a modest little cottage that looked as if it might contain no more than three rooms. It was on entering the cottage that Dirksen received his first surprise. In the living room was a Bechstein grand piano, an instrument nine feet long and generally known as the "Rolls Royce" of pianos. It was not the piano of Bossanyi, but it belonged to his wife who was a concert pianist. A tiny little woman, quite elderly, she could still play beautifully.

With his heavy snow white hair, Bossanyi reminded Dirksen of Franz Liszt, the Hungarian pianist. The artist was a thoughtful host, and saw to it that Dirksen enjoyed a cup of tea. After the refreshments, Bossanyi led Dirksen out in the back of his home to a small shed that was his studio. He provided a small keg for Dirksen to sit on, similar to the kegs used for nails in this country in the past, and then turned on lights in the shed. Dirksen saw three pulldown window shades that were obviously hiding something. When the lights were properly adjusted, Bossanyi raised first the right shade, then the left and finally the center shade to disclose the three lancets of his window, "War and Peace". This was the window that was to be placed in the Woodrow Wilson Bay at Washington National Cathedral, and it is known as his greatest work.

Dirksen was the first cathedral employee to see the completed window and the recollection of that occasion is still fresh in his memory.

Dedication of the Nave, July 1976.
Left to right, Prince Philip, the late Bishop
John Walker and First Lady Betty Ford,
all led by Verger John Kraus.
The Verger always leads.

Cathedral Archives

The Prince Evaluates the Verger

On one of his visits to Washington, His Royal Highness Prince Charles came to the cathedral to participate in a service. On this occasion, he was to read one of the lessons from the lectern. As in all services, the Verger leads the person to the place where he or she is to read and also instructs the person on the protocol for the occasion. The Verger is the person in charge; and of all participants it is he who is the last authority on the order of the service.

When it became time for Prince Charles to read the lesson, the Verger, John Kraus, came to his chair and led him to the steps at the lectern. The Verger had instructed the Prince to walk up to the lectern, wait three seconds, and then read. When he had completed the reading, the Verger led him back to his seat again.

That evening at a dinner party, Prince Charles spoke to friends about his trip and what in his visit to America had most impressed him. With wry good humor, he mentioned that he found the Verger at Washington National Cathedral to be a very decisive person who knew precisely what the Prince was to do, when he was to do it, and when he was to return to his seat. He thought it would be invaluable to have such a person always at hand. This, among other after-dinner remarks, appeared in the following day's news accounts of the Prince's activities.

But now, unfortunately for the cathedral and unfortunately for Prince Charles, should he return, Verger John Kraus has retired, having performed his duties at Washington National Cathedral for 25 years. He received congratulatory letters from Queen Elizabeth II, Presidents Reagan, Bush and Clinton on his retirement.

The Wandering Choir

The procession is a part of all Episcopal services. It is always an impressive part of the service and establishes the formal introduction of the religious drama that is to follow. Processions do not just happen. They are planned in great detail. For example, there must be a specific place for each person in the procession to sit. These things cannot be left to chance.

For some special services, such as the consecration of a bishop or a special diocesan service with many visiting choirs, the processions become quite long. Even a normal Sunday with a choir of 50 voices, the attending clergy, the acolytes, lay readers—all of whom are led by the Verger—a substantial number of persons are involved.

Dirksen recalls one Sunday about 1967 when the Cathedral Choral Society was to sing later in the day. This required not only bleachers to be set up to accommodate the singers, but chairs for the full orchestra that was to accompany them. This was, of course, at the time when the nave was under construction and the west wall enclosed only three bays of the present nave. Typically, the choir would process from the north transept, down the north nave aisle to the west end, cross over to the south nave aisle and then process to the Great Choir.

The processional began in good order. The procession came down to the west end ready to turn over to the south aisle, but the area was jammed full of bleachers and chairs for the Choral Society and there was no place for them to go. Demonstrating a rare degree of initiative and inventiveness, the choir merely left the nave through the west end door at the end of the aisle, crossed over on the construction site outside and re-entered the Cathedral at the south aisle west entrance.

Paul Callaway was at the organ and Dirksen was standing at his side turning the pages. Callaway had been listening carefully to the choir as it sang the hymn, but was puzzled when the sound dwindled and disappeared entirely.

Turning to Dirksen, he asked, "Where did the choir go?"

Dirksen who had witnessed the entire debacle was laughing so hard that he could hardly manage to reply, "Outside, Paul."

Callaway's response was terse, censorious, and did not constitute a direct quote from scripture. Imagine his surprise when the choir entered again at the south aisle entrance to the west, still singing in time and in tune. They finally arrived at the Great Choir stalls. Nothing of this kind of procession could have been planned and performed as well. The Dean is reported to have informed the Verger that he didn't think highly of this procession and he hoped that the Canon Precentor had not been responsible for it. The Canon Precentor was also mystified about the procession and disclaimed any instructions given for it. But then, it could well be that both the Dean and the Canon Precentor wished secretly that they had thought of the entire procedure themselves.

The Musician Tries His Hand at Golf

Dirksen's sons became concerned with the constancy of their father's occupation. They believed that he should have some kind of recreation and relief from his work. The idea of golf appealed to them. After all, Dirksen had a very powerful athletic build. He ought to be a whiz at the game.

Acquiring a set of clubs, Dirksen undertook to learn this new game. He was a master at playing the Great Organ at the cathedral, he certainly should be a good golfer; playing golf obviously was not as complex as playing an organ.

Dirksen went to a driving range several times and felt he understood the mechanics of driving the ball. He went out on a course and played a round or so. Things were going rather well. He felt ready to play.

A foursome was arranged for very early one Saturday morning. Dirksen was going to play with Roger Morigi, the cathedral's Master Stone Carver. What a pair they would make together! Morigi was 5' 3" tall and weighed 125 on a heavy day. But he could drive a golf ball and played with a very low handicap. Dirksen was 6'4" and weighed 220 on a light day. The other two were Jack Fanfani, a cathedral employee and Geoffrey, Dirksen's son.

At the first tee, Dirksen was to drive off first. He surveyed the fairway, measured his stance to the ball, checked his grip, brought his driver back in a beautiful backstroke and then swung through missing the ball entirely. That was not what he had intended to do.

Feeling somewhat embarrassed he began to re-set himself when he was aware of some activity behind him and when he looked, both his son and Fanfani were lying on the ground laughing. Only Morigi looked composed. That could only mean one thing.

"What did you say?" Dirksen asked Morigi.

Morigi replied forthrightly, "I just told them that you were the great musician at the cathedral who never missed a note, but on the golf course you missed the whole damned piano!"

Jane K. L. Miller

Jane K. L. Miller was born at the United States Military Academy, at West Point, New York where her father, a professional Army officer, was a member of the faculty. She loved the excitement, the movings and meetings of military life and she also married a professional Army officer. They are the proud parents of five daughters. Due to both her father's and husband's careers, Jane has lived in 28 locations in the United States, the Philippines and Europe, including 16 years in Germany and France.

Placed in positions of increasing distaff responsibility, Jane worked in various leadership roles in American military communities in Europe. Her expertise and interests focused around the areas of community volunteerism and the management of nursery and child care facilities. She wrote and spoke widely on these topics. Jane came to the cathedral in 1983 as a docent. In 1987 she became the cathedral's fourth Director of Visitor Services. In September 1993, this department was expanded and her title was changed to Director, Visitor Programs and Volunteer Services. As such, she supervises not only the old Department of Visitor Services, but also Area School Programs, the Medieval Workshop and the Office of the Coordinator of Volunteers. She is responsible for programs for visitors of all ages, (to include six created since 1988), and has oversight of the interpretation of the cathedral to over 600,000 visitors a year as well as the cathedral volunteers who make this and many other cathedral programs possible. In 1992-93, she served on the Search Committee for the new Dean of Washington National Cathedral.

Jane's special interests include art and architecture (especially Gothic), genealogy, American and European history and culture, and public speaking.

The following selected stories represent notations that have been recorded by the docents in the Docents' Log of their experiences with visitors to the cathedral. These have been augmented by some of Jane's personal recollections.

80

Bulgarian Women

It was shortly after the Berlin Wall had come down when a group of Bulgarian women who were touring the United States came to visit the cathedral. They had been given a tour and at the conclusion asked if they could sing in the nave. Not infrequently, visiting choirs and groups do sing while visiting the cathedral and so the docents were pleased to agree to their request. What they heard was something truly unusual and beautiful.

The women separated and stood at a distance from each other around the crossing. First one would sing a few measures and then another at some distance would take up the refrain and add another few measures. A third would follow and then others, until all had participated; then they would begin again and repeat the same routine. This, the docents understood, was the way the women in Bulgaria sang together while working in the fields.

The Log describes the experience as "hauntingly beautiful and truly distinctive." What a shame it could not have been recorded.

Ervin Bossanyi

One of the great joys of the docents is in meeting people from all parts of the world who in turn bring stories of an association with the cathedral previously unknown. A visitor from Australia talked with the docents at length about the stained-glass artist Ervin Bossanyi. Mr. Bossanyi had created the glowing War and Peace Window in the Wilson Bay, and the National Cathedral Association Window on the north side of the nave. Born in Hungary in 1891, he had emigrated to Germany to pursue his artistic interests but was forced to move again since he was of the Jewish faith. He had then fled to England in 1934.

The visitor had lived next door to Bossanyi in England and had helped him in his studio. He had crated windows for shipment to their destination and had performed other odd jobs. He said that Bossanyi did all of the work on his windows himself, including both design and fabrication. Nothing was sub-contracted to other studios. He described Bossanyi as looking the part of an artist, always wearing a beret and an old coat. Interestingly, not only was he a stained- glass artist, he also painted pictures and was a collecter of lace. His work reflected the cultures of all of the countries where he had lived.

Our Amish Visitors

Late on July 5, 1988, a large delegation of Amish visited from Indiana. They represented all generations, small children to very elderly men with long snow-white beards. All were simply dressed in their typical way and the women wore the small white lace prayer coverings on their heads.

They were asked if they sang in their church. In response, one man sang a few notes and with that they all began to sing a lovely German hymn. Every one of the visitors sang. Although their demeanor was somber, they sang with feeling and with reverence.

The Last Gargoyle

The Docents' Log for December 17, 1987 records, "Another milestone day, clear but windy and frigid! Workmen, Bishop, Provost, Canons, Staff, Cathedral friends, TV and other media people, climbed the north tower to observe the setting of the last gargoyle."

Jane Miller has vivid memories of the occasion. She remembers climbing up those many steps to the top of the tower and she was grateful that she had dressed warmly. "When we got to the top," she recalls, "I was surprised to see so many people already there. It was truly awesome! There was no parapet, only some wire around the edge of the platform to urge people away. The city seemed a long way down.

The last gargoyle set at the Washington Cathedral. Mason Foreman Joe Alonzo, on the left, with mason's helper Gilbert Davis.

Photo: Cathedral Public Affairs

"A slight distance away on another platform, I remember seeing the sculptor, a very young Jay Carpenter, standing, looking at his handiwork—the last gargoyle. It was huge—a caveman holding a bone in his hand. I thought Jay looked ill at ease at that altitude, or perhaps I was merely transferring my own concern to him. It was an exciting experience to look down from that height on the city of Washington spread out around us and to realize that we were seeing something truly memorable; the setting of the last gargoyle on the Washington Cathedral, 80 years after the laying of the foundation stone."

Walker Hancock's Model

In September 1988, the docents recorded a visit by a young couple, Mr. and Mrs. Robert Greel. After the tour, they asked to see the Chapel of the Good Shepherd. Many years previously, Mr. Greel said he had posed for Walker Hancock with a pillow in his arm, while Mr. Hancock worked on the sculpture that now graces that chapel.

The docent who accompanied them said that it was very obvious Mr. Greel had sat for the sculpture since the similarity of facial features was easy to discern. Greel had also posed for the Christ in Majesty sculpture, central to the High Altar reredos, sitting with his right hand raised and a small ball in his left hand.

The Daughter of Toyohiko Kagawa

The daughter of the Reverend Toyohiko Kagawa, a very well known Japanese evangelist, social worker and writer, was with a group visiting the cathedral. She was employed in a corporation that was participating in a seminar at Wesley Theological Seminary where she had delivered an address. Since it had been 100 years since Kagawa's birth, the group thought it would be appropriate to observe the occasion by coming to see his statue in the Bettelheim Bay, north aisle.

Unfortunately, the daughter said that the statue we have at the cathedral does not at all resemble her father. This is not surprising. Family members or close friends seldom ever find works of art to be accurate. It might even be observed, that the only sculptures or paintings that are considered truly accurate, are those of subjects who have been dead for at least a century along with those who knew them personally.

Master Carver Roger Morigi carving the reredos for the Chapel of the Good Shepherd.
The sculptor was Walter Hancock.

Prime Minister de Mazaire Visits

Some time during the breakup of the East European Communist governments, Prime Minister de Mazaire of East Germany came to visit the cathedral. At the time it had been an unusual experience to have a visitor from an avowed communist country. Jane Miller remembers him as being small of stature and absolutely charming. She described him as having a nice smile, a firm handshake and a pleasant personality. He spoke no English but he had an interpreter with him. He said that he was a musician. He played the violin and was interested in anything to do with music. His daughter, he said, was also a musician.

Canon Michael Hamilton and Jane met him and gave him a tour of the cathedral. He appeared very interested and said that he was a Christian. When the tour was completed and he returned to his embassy car, Hamilton leaned in, shook his hand and said that he would be praying for him and for his people. He was obviously very touched by this, and he waved to his two hosts until his car was out of sight.

"Some time later," recalls Jane, "we read in the news that he had been accused by his enemies of being an informer against his own people during the communist period. I found these charges hard to accept after meeting and talking with the man in person."

A Wedding Ruckus!

The wedding was scheduled for two P.M. It was a large affair; six bridesmaids, three junior bridesmaids, one flower girl, one junior flower girl, and one ring bearer. The procession was to start at the west doors and that's where the trouble began.

+ The principals were late, everything got started at 2:25.

+ The bride's train was 30 feet long, a cascade of ruffles, described as looking like soap bubbles.

+ The ring bearer tossed the pillow as he walked down the aisle.

+ The junior flower girl fell on the steps and dropped her bouquet. When she ran to recover the bouquet, the ring bearer tripped the flower girl.

+ An usher dropped his boutonniere during the procession and stopped to pick it up.

It is recorded that everything in the cathedral remained cool throughout except the Verger's temper!

*Kneeling statue of
President Abraham Lincoln
by Herbert Houck.
The statue is at the Parclose Stairs.*

Lincoln, by Houck

A group of visitors from St. Stephens Cathedral in Harrisburg, Pennsylvania, asked to see the statue of Abraham Lincoln kneeling in prayer, that is placed at the top of the Parclose Stairs. They reminded the docent, that the sculpture was originally among those submitted to be considered for the Lincoln Memorial in Washington. The sculpture had been the work of Herbert Houck who had been a member of St. Stephens in Harrisburg. When the work had not been accepted for the memorial, the small statue was sent to Washington Cathedral for permanent retention.

The Dalai Lama

Jane Miller is not likely to forget this day. "We had expected a large crowd to see the Dalai Lama," she recalls, "but nothing to compare with what actually developed. People began arriving very early and saving seats for their friends. They brought bouquets of flowers and other gifts that they wanted to give to this holy man. Long before the scheduled service, every seat was taken and the nave was full. It was then that the cathedral doors had to be closed and explanations made to late-comers that fire regulations prohibited any one else from entering.

"I was asked to stand outside of the main west doors and to help explain this requirement. The audio was to be piped outdoors so that everyone could at least hear what was going on but no one else could be allowed to enter. What a crowd! People came forward with all sorts of identification to tell me how important they were: that they were diplomats, that they were members of the Dalai Lama's personal staff, that they were members of the Dalai Lama's family. On that occasion, he was probably related to at least several hundred persons! I fully expected to be offered bribes to let a few more enter."

When the service was finally over and the Dalai Lama started to recess toward the west doors, everyone began to press forward wanting to touch him. It was quite an experience for the Security Officers and those helping them to restrain the crowd that tried to reach him. There was concern that he might be injured.

Jane recalls the occasion with a look of relief that there was no major incident. "He was a very handsome man," she adds, "much younger in appearance than I expected and with a look of physical strength. His neck especially seemed to be very strong and well developed, like the neck of a wrestler."

Omnium-gatherum

Dr. Thomas McKnew came by for a visit. Dr. McKnew sang in the choir as a youth on the occasion when the cathedral foundation stone was set in 1907. He later served as the first construction company superintendent during the time that the apse was built. Dr. McKnew, who had a long association with the National Geographic Society, was a great benefactor of the cathedral and served as a member of the Building Committee.

✚

On the day before the observance of his birthday, a tiny girl stood on tip-toe to kiss the shoe of the statue of Abraham Lincoln.

A woman requested the docents to let her run up and down the tower stairs since she was preparing for a mountain climbing experience in Nepal. No notation has been recorded indicating that she either did run up the stairs in the tower or that she climbed a mountain in Nepal.

A gentleman from North Carolina came to find a Brenda Belfield window for which he had made some glass. It was found in the northwest turret, facing north, and he was very glad to see how the glass had been employed. The egg-shaped pieces of glass, he told us, have layers of silver that show gold in the daylight and blue-green at night.

For years, it was commonly accepted that the construction yard in front of the cathedral, where many construction stones were laid out waiting to be built into the cathedral fabric, was actually a cemetery where a number of people were buried.

A teacher with her sixth grade class, asked a Docent to "Tell the class about the 90-year-old carver who lives in the shack out front" (referring to one of the construction buildings in front of the cathedral). Oddly enough, this was a request that was heard often before the cathedral was finished, but no one knows where or why it originated.

A woman visitor, enthralled by the reflections of the stained-glass windows on the floor and walls asked, "Where do you keep the lights that make these beautiful colors?"

A sixth grade youth came up to the docent station and asked how the organ pipes were taken out of the organ to be played. He had assumed that the pipes were played much as a recorder or flute might be played by a piper; one picked them up in one's hands and played them

In October 1988, we had a visit from a number of Jewish Canadians. They said they had visited many cathedrals in Europe but they felt Washington Cathedral to be one of the most beautiful, so open, so lovely and they felt so very much at home. They were especially intrigued by the ten stones in the floor in front of the High Altar that were taken from Mount Sinai, showing that our priests stand firmly on the Ten Commandments here when they celebrate from the High Altar.

The grandson and great-granddaughter of Dr. Wilfred T. Grenfell, a medical missionary to Labrador, visited the cathedral and asked to see the Physician's Window. Dr. Grenfell had been pictured in the right lancet. The window is in the east clerestory of the north transept.

Early in 1989 a young couple called and wanted to see the sculpture of Bishop Samuel Isaac Joseph Schereschewsky. He had been born a Russian Jew, later became an Anglican priest, was elevated to become the Bishop of Shanghai and translated the Bible into Mandarin Chinese. He was the young woman's great-grandfather. They were delighted to be able to photograph his statue in the reredos at the High Altar. She said her grandmother had told her so many stories of her great-grandfather that he had always remained something of a mythical figure until that moment.

A woman visitor said that she was most disappointed in the restrooms at the cathedral in that they were not Gothic. If, however, the cathedral had chosen to build restrooms typical of the early Gothic period of the 13th century, she might have been even more disappointed in them!

We always view any situation or circumstance from a perspective that is familiar to us. A British couple, familiar with English cathedrals that have been there for centuries, remarked to the docent, "You have done a remarkable job of cleaning up the place."

Clare Yellin, the grandaughter of Samuel Yellin, renowned wrought-iron artisan, visited the cathedral in January 1990. She was accompanied by a blacksmith from England. They were interested in seeing the wrought-iron work by Samuel Yellin and the other wrought-iron artists.

✚

We were paid a visit by Peg Whistler Roberts who had served as one of the three drafts persons for Philip Hubert Frohman, the Cathedral Architect. She came to the cathedral with her husband, General Roberts. She told us she had designed the lettering in stone for the cathedral offices as well as one of the baptismal fonts. She confirmed what we already knew: that Mr. Frohman was a meticulous task-master. The drafts persons were required to make a full-size drawing of each stone on which they worked before final approval could be given for any carving.

✚

In June 1988, two groups visited representing the Peacewalk. Many of those from the Soviet Union identified themselves as Christians and gave the docents medals that commemorated the millenium celebration being held in that country. These were not really unique groups; since that time there have been many visits of persons from Russia and other former Soviet Republics.

In the earlier days, these visitors seemed to display very little emotion about the visit or show little interest in the building. After the break-up of the Soviet Union, however, the Russian visitors have been much less stoic and have expressed a great amount of interest in the cathedral and what it stands for. There now are so many Russian visitors that the touring brochure has been translated and printed in Russian with references to personages or events with which they may identify.

A couple from Ohio began an annual pilgrimage 20 years ago to the gravesites of all of America's deceased presidents. In June 1988 they came to the cathedral to visit the tomb of Woodrow Wilson. They had by that time visited all of the former presidents' gravesites except for Polk in Tennessee and Buchanan in Pennsylvania.

It is always interesting for docents to see the cathedral through the eyes of their visitors, especially when those visitors are artists. In the fall of 1988, Heinrich Jarcgyk who had a collection on exhibit in Washington, visited the cathedral with his Swiss wife. He was a German-born Pole. The two were quite excited and even enchanted by the cathedral. Specifically, they noted Rowan LeCompte's West Rose Window that they thought magnificent, that Lawrence Saint's windows were very like medieval glass, Frederick Hart's tympanums were superb, Rodney Winfield's Space Window caught the energy and emotion of space and they felt we were very brave to attempt a cathedral in the 20th century.

A visitor just before Christmas 1988, told an interesting but unverifiable story. In the 1930s, his mother was to meet James Edward Freeman, the third Bishop of the Washington Diocese, at Union Station and to drive him to the cathedral. When the Bishop discovered that the car was to be driven by a woman, he proclaimed that he had never ridden in a car with a woman driver and he did not intend to do so then! How fortunate, that Bishop Freeman was the Diocesan during the 30s and not the 90s.

Mrs. Colin Powell came one morning soon after the Persian Gulf War escorting a group of South American visitors. She said that she and her husband felt a very close association with the cathedral since their son had been baptized in the Children's Chapel.

Margaret Truman Daniels came to the cathedral for a meeting but afterwards wanted to wander on her own. She was offered the lounge where she could rest and she took advantage of that. She was no stranger to the cathedral, having had a close relationship with the National Cathedral Association. In this instance the docents surmised that she was doing research for her book, *Murder in the Cathedral.*

Imelda Marcos came to a funeral and the cathedral was jammed when she arrived. A seat was finally found for her, over in the north nave aisle. True to form, everyone looked at her shoes as she was known to have many pairs, and they were something to behold; the very high heels were alternating stripes of black and bright gold.

✛

Art Linkletter was an early morning visitor, and was shown around by one of the docents. He said that he had been a "PK" (a preacher's kid). He was especially taken with the John the Baptist window.

✛

Prime Minister Mulrooney, the Prime Minister of Canada with his secret service entourage came by. He did not tour but asked a number of questions about the cathedral and said he thought it was a beautiful building.

A Praying Mantis

Soon after she began as a cathedral employee, Jane Miller decided that it would be important for her to "experience" the position where the volunteers work. Accordingly, one evening she came to the nave to help host the cathedral during the extended summer hours. Some of the visitors had been taken up to the observation gallery in order to view the exterior of the cathedral as well as the city of Washington from the windows so far above the ground.

Along with one group was a young boy, about eight years old, who returned from the gallery and went to the desk in the west end where Jane was standing. It was obvious that he was excited about something he had in his hand. When he had Jane's attention he opened his hand, and in it was an enormous praying mantis. "Look," he said. "I found him on a window ledge in the gallery. See, he's praying. He knows this is a church too!"

The Joe Garagiola Dollar Bill

A tour director of a group from Los Angeles rushed back into the cathedral after her group had already boarded the bus, to explain that she had received a dollar bill autographed by Joe Garagiola of the "Today" television show, and by mistake, had dropped it into the cathedral contribution box. The key was obtained and with several docents on their knees going through the money, the bill was found and returned to the woman who ran to her bus, breathless but happy!

Now, it is not unusual to see people on their knees in the cathedral—but in front of the contribution box?

Queen Elizabeth and Prince Philip

This was one experience that Jane Miller would not soon forget. "How exciting!" she recalls. "I have never seen such a level of excitment on the part of the public. People were lined up early and trying to get into the nave to get a better seat. Actually, a visit by the president is pretty mild in comparison to the excitment that is generated by a visit from Queen Elizabeth II of England."

Queen Elizabeth had been to the cathedral several times, most recently at the Bicentennial celebration, so this was not a new experience for her. The "reception committee" waited in the narthex, the "committee" consisting of Bishop Haines, Interim Provost Garner, Margot Semler, the Verger, the other clergy and Jane Miller. They had told Jane that she was to be a part of the procession, that she was to walk near the Queen and if the Queen wanted to ask a question, Jane would be the person to respond, but she had not taken this very seriously. "I could not believe that the Queen would ask anything of me or that I would have the opportunity to speak to her. It was a lovely honor but I was sure the Queen would never ask a touring type any question."

"We greeted our guests, I shook the Queen's white-gloved hand and was pleased with myself that I remembered the proper protocol in addressing her. She was much prettier than in her pictures, with very bright, warm, blue eyes. We lined up very quickly to process down the center aisle in the nave, (the official party had been late arriving) and lo and behold, everyone else had fallen to the back. The Queen was now flanked by Margot Semler on the left and by me on the right!"

They walked very slowly down the aisle to the front of the cathedral and Queen Elizabeth turned and asked Jane two questions as they walked, one about the Space Window and the other about President Wilson's tomb. Fortunately, Jane knew the answers to both. When they got to the Crossing, a gift was given to the Queen and she in turn gave a Bible to Provost Garner. He was very pleased by this and the gift was placed on exhibit in the Rare Book Library for some time.

"We went up to the Great Choir" recalls Jane, "and Queen Elizabeth and Prince Philip knelt for prayers in front of the High Altar, she using the needlepoint cushion that had been completed by her mother, Queen Mary. After the brief service, they processed to the north transept and out to their motorcade. It was altogether a short occasion, probably under half an hour, but so memorable to all of us there that day."

Joan Baez and James Taylor Concert

Jane Miller had not been employed at the cathedral for very long when she heard that Joan Baez and James Taylor would be performing there at an evening benefit sponsored by Amnesty International. "I thought this would be a very interesting experience," she says, "and I called my daughter Katey, who was then a high school senior, and she came to the cathedral to join me. At the time, Marjorie

Pawlitz, my assistant, and I were sharing space in a small glass-walled room inside the larger Houghton Volunteer Center. There were two desks in the glass-enclosed area; a very small space to accommodate us."

Jane had not anticipated that the two performers would need space to wait before the performance or that the Volunteer Center would be selected as the waiting room. Marjorie, Katey and Jane crowded into the little glass-walled office trying to appear as if they were busy with many things. James Taylor tuned his guitar while the rest of the group thumbed through the supply of magazines and enjoyed cups of coffee.

At last the concert started and the nave was jammed. The high point of the concert for Jane as well as for others, was hearing Joan Baez sing "Amazing Grace" without any accompaniment as she walked very slowly from the west end up the center nave aisle to the Crossing.

The Rare Book Library Exhibit Room

In 1988, the Office of Visitor Services undertook some projects to attract new audiences to view displays of the cathedral's rare books and artifacts from the storage rooms and archives. Some exhibits were arranged that have featured beautiful and ornate vestments, altar vessels and linens, photographs of memorable occasions, interesting letters, some of the exquisite rare books in the collection. Other exhibits have featured simple mementos of interesting items that have accumulated over the years. These valuable treasures have been given to the cathedral by many donors and it was only proper that they should be shared with the public.

The first exhibit was one honoring our presidents. From the cathedral archives photographs of presidents were obtained, and an exhibit was mounted using one of the pictures for each president of the United States since the cathedral received its charter from congress in 1893. It was a modest little exhibit but it was good to have it on display during the presidential election in 1988.

One of the more satisfying exhibits was one emphasizing the work of Marian Lane, a lady who had designed many of the cathedral Christmas cards over the years. The cathedral had been offered a collection of her exquisitely detailed work by a friend of the cathedral who had received a collection of Marian Lane designs at the time of her death. The exhibit included a collection of calligraphy that incorporated not only the borrowed items, but a complete assembling of her designs for cards that had been misplaced here at the cathedral for some years.

We accrued an unanticipated bonus through this exhibit. The cathedral now has the names and addresses of many people owning originals of Ms. Lane's work. Not only did she complete many exquisite designs for cards, she also produced some beautiful hand-tooled book covers and illuminations.

The Visitors' Lounge

The entrance area to the Resurrection Chapel and to St. Dunstan's Chapel was not one of the more inviting areas in the cathedral. We decided that we could improve it by making it into a welcoming lounge for visitors. We had the place painted and in order to soften the sound and also add some color, with the assistance of the National Cathedral Association, we obtained and placed all of the state flags that are now on display in the lounge. This also serves to draw attention to the state books that are at this location for visitors to sign, if they wish to do so.

Now we can tell visitors that each state is represented at least four times in the cathedral: the state books that are maintained here for visitors to sign, the state flags that hang both in the nave at the clerestory level and in the visitors' center, and the state seals in the floor of the narthex.

New Tour Opportunities

Visitor Programs has instituted two new tour opportunities that are open to the public and that have proved to be very well received. These are the Close-up Tour and the Tea and Tour.

The Close-up Tour is fashioned after the Painting-of-the-Week tour that is offered by many galleries and it was, at first, offered on each Sunday. The idea behind this tour was to attract visitors to the cathedral on a regular basis, and to enable us to obtain repeat, local audiences. We developed a long list of subjects on which a great amount of research was done, resulting in very detailed presentations. The tours were very successful but because they entailed a tremendous amount of work on the part of our docents we had to reduce the scope of our activity. Now the tours are offered only on the first Sunday of the month and they are limited to the specialty tours that we have available, i.e., Stained Glass, Architecture, Needlepoint, Symbolism and other similar subjects. These tours had been available for a long time but were offered only to special interest groups that requested them. Now the general public may also enjoy them.

The Tea and Tour program was developed jointly between All Hallows Guild and Visitor Services. Each of the two would accept responsibility for a portion of the program and would receive some of the benefits. The program was described in several publications and attracted such attention that now reservations have flooded in and the tours are booked for as much as six months in advance.

Roger Morigi

Photo by H. Byron Chambers

Roger Morigi was born in Italy in 1907 at Bisuschio, a small village about three miles from the Swiss border. His home was midway between Lake Como and Lake Lugano, in one of the most beautiful areas in the world. He lived at home, going to the local elementary school during his early years and transferring afterwards to the Brera Academy in Milan. He stayed there for ten years, studying to become a stone carver, and taking classes in drawing, structures, construction and modeling. He won two gold medals for charcoal drawing and was subsequently apprenticed to the artists Castiglianoni and Violi who supervised his work on a number of monuments.

In 1927 when he was 20, he joined his father, Napoleon Morigi, a well established stone carver working in Connecticut. With no knowledge of English he took a ship to New York and then managed to get the train to New Haven where he joined his father. The very first thing he did, according to Roger, was to visit the Post Office and apply for his citizenship papers. He worked for his father for nine months to demonstrate his proficiency as a stone carver, and during this time he attended night school to learn to speak English. At the conclusion of this time, he accepted a position with John Donnelly, a nationally known stone carving contractor in New York. He worked on projects at Grand Central Station, Rockefeller Center, and Riverside Church. His work may also be found at the State Capitol in Charleston, West Virginia, and at Duke University in Durham, North Carolina. He earned $14 a day as a stone carver which was a very high salary in the late 1920s.

In the early 1930s, Morigi was sent to Washington where he worked on the Post Office at 12th and Pennsylvania Avenue, the American Pharmaceutical Association Building, the Court of Appeals for the District of Columbia, and the Federal Courthouse. For several years he worked on the new Supreme Court Building. He recalled that from the construction site he was able to take photographs of President Franklin D. Roosevelt at his inauguration in 1933.

In 1952, Morigi came to the cathedral and stayed there for 28 years until his retirement in 1980. Very shortly after coming to the cathedral, he was promoted to Master Carver and given the responsibility to supervise all of the other stone carvers. He described his time at the cathedral as the happiest of his life.

In 1936, Morigi had married Louise Kavakof, a union that lasted 58 years. There are two children of whom he was justifiably proud, a daughter Elaine who is a vice president of Citizen's Bank of Maryland and a son Francis who is Chairman of the Art Department at Syracuse University. Roger and his wife lived at their home in Hyattsville, Maryland, where they were surrounded by pictures and mementos of the many honors that came to Roger over the years. He passed away in January 1995 at the age of 87.

"A stone carver is inclined to be an honest man," said Morigi with a twinkle in his eye. "An executive may embellish his resume but a stone carver's work is there for all to see. No matter how well he writes, it does not change the quality of his carving."

Morigi's Early Life in New York

Morigi spoke wistfully of his early days in New York during the late 1920s. He talked about life in Greenwich Village and in the Bronx, where he lived. There was a sense of community in the Village where most of the residents were writers, artists, sculptors, musicians—all people who respected each other and each others' talents. Because of this mutual respect, he added, there was no crime. Everyone felt safe.

There was a large Italian community in New York and they enjoyed each others' company. Saturday night was a special night where friends would meet, play cards or just converse, usually with a glass of wine. There was no effective prohibition, said Morigi, but the use of spirits was seldom abused. Saturday night was the community's recreation.

One friend of Morigi's lingered in his memory. Every week, the same ritual would be played out and always with the same results. His friend would leave home to go out with "the boys" and his wife would ask him, "Will you be home early tonight?"

"Oh yes," he would reply. "By 11:30 for sure."

The group would begin their card playing, conversation and banter and always the friend would look at his watch at 11:45 and say, "Oh my! I didn't make it home by 11:30." Then he would shrug his shoulders and add, "So since I am late, now I can stay out as long as I want."

The Supreme Court Building

Several years ago, Roger Morigi was asked to take Justice Sandra Day O'Connor through the Supreme Court Building and describe processes of the building's construction, but especially to emphasize the many works of art including those that he had accomplished. As they went around the building, he pointed out the stone carvings for which he had been responsible:

✦ In the southwest court, a frieze along the roofline of the building consisting of a series of cornucopia that extend for the full length of the court, a distance of over 100 feet.

✦ The tympanum over the eastern entrance to the building representing those great civilizations in the East that have made contributions to the fundamental laws and precepts that influence our own civilization. The three central figures are of Moses the Law Giver, flanked by Confucius and Solon. These figures are in turn flanked by symbolical figures representing enforcement of the law, tempering justice with mercy, the presence of youth to signify the carrying on of our civilization through aquiring a knowledge of right and wrong. The sculptor who created the model for the tympanum was Herman A. MacNeil.

✦ One of the lamp posts, one of the Corinthian capitals, and the left side of the main west entrance to the building.

Toward the end of the visit, Morigi turned to his guest and said, "Madam Justice, I mean no disrespect, but you are looking at me in a very strange manner. I wonder if I have said something that you may not have understood."

"No," she replied. "It is just that I have been aware of what a great privilege this tour has been. When I have visited great works of art in Italy that were done centuries ago, I have often wondered how the artists appeared. What did they look like? Here in this building that I love, I can look at the many works of art that are so pleasing to me and I shall always be reminded that I have met and known the artist!"

Working With Mr. Frohman

When Morigi first came to the cathedral, the architect Philip Hubert Frohman would come twice each day to see what he was doing. After two weeks, the visits dropped off to once each day and then not at all. This disturbed Morigi because he wanted to be sure he was doing his work the way it was expected of him and he was unable to reassure himself when he could not speak with Frohman. It was not long, however, before Morigi was told to proceed on his own and he did not receive any direct supervision.

In 1954 when Morigi was named the Master Carver at Washington Cathedral, he was perplexed when Mr. Frohman began coming to him and asking his opinion on certain drawings and details that Frohman was preparing.

"Why do you come to see me and ask my opinion?" he questioned Frohman. "My knowledge of architecture and construction is no more than a mere fraction of your knowledge."

"Ah, but you are wrong," replied Frohman. "Because four eyes always see much better than two."

What Morigi did not understand at the time, was that Frohman respected his artistic ability and truly valued his judgment. It was a good relationship that lasted until Frohman retired.

New Year's Eve

Bottles remaining from the Stone Carvers' New Year's Eve Observances.

Morigi does not remember which year it was but it was shortly after he had become the Master Carver. On December 31, all of the carvers had come to work as usual and had gone to their appointed tasks. Morigi went to see each of them and told them that at noon that day they would stop for lunch and then they would have a glass of champagne, that Morigi had purchased, to celebrate the arrival of the new year. Thereafter, by mid-afternoon, they would all be given the rest of the day as a holiday although they would be paid for a full work day.

It must have been about two o'clock and they were all seated around the carver's shack enjoying the camaraderie of the occasion, when the door to the shack flew open with a loud crash, and there stood Dean Sayre, his arms folded over his chest and a very stern look on his face. Morigi remembers the shack suddenly becoming very quiet, everyone apprehensive about what the Dean would say.

What the Dean said was, "So, where is my glass?"

At the insistence of Dean Sayre, Morigi got a sheet of paper, had each carver sign his name, put the date on the paper and pasted it to one of the bottles. That bottle was preserved as a keepsake for the carvers. Every year since that time, a bottle has been saved to commemorate the occasion shared by all the carvers at the cathedral.

Relationship with the Dean

Morigi spoke wistfully of the many friends he had at the cathedral and the fact that he liked all of them. When it came to Dean Sayre, however, he felt the emotion was much stronger. "I love that man," he said.

Dean Sayre knew every workman by name, whether he was a mason, carver or laborer. Whatever his task, the Dean knew him and always spoke to him. Every spring, after the hiatus over the winter months, Sayre would go around to each man to welcome him back on the job at the cathedral, to inquire about his health and to ask about his family.

After the first party for New Year's Eve, the Dean came to Morigi and asked when there would be another party of the workmen. He encouraged Morigi to think of some reason for all to get together, knowing that it would be good for the workmen's morale. They did have parties periodically and they became so crowded that it was necessary to move from the carver's shack to one of the school dining rooms.

Working with an Artist

When he became the Master Carver at the cathedral, Morigi was always looking for new talent. There were some very fine stone carvers at the cathedral but there was always room for another one, especially if he had real talent.

He found one! At least, Morigi was very impressed with what the young man was doing. He had a studio (actually, an old garage) on a back alley in Washington where he lived with his two big dogs and where he did his work. From what Morigi could see, the young artist didn't have the price of a hamburger and he wondered how he could survive. But his work as a sculptor was impressive.

Morigi invited the young man to come to the cathedral and he would give him some instruction in stone carving. The young man was a quick learner and before long he was doing acceptable work. Very soon, he was given freedom to begin work carving a gargoyle. After several days, Morigi started climbing the scaffolding to see how the young man was progressing. As he neared the work site, he was aware that there was no activity, the young man was leaning on the hand rail, smoking a cigarette and staring off into space.

"I don't hear any noise from stone carving," said Morigi.

The young man looked at Morigi and replied, "Stone carvers make noise; artists dream."

"For the first time in my life I was at a loss for words," said Morigi. Anyone who knew this effusive and gregarious man knows that it could not have happened often. So he turned around, descended the scaffolding and said nothing more.

The young man? He was Frederick Hart. Today he is one of the foremost sculptors in America. In addition to his sculptures of Adam, St. Peter and St. Paul at the west front portals of the cathedral, he also is the artist for the three west portal tympanums. He is well known for the three soldiers at the Vietnam Veteran's Memorial as well as many beautiful acrylic and other sculptures that he has done commercially.

One has to agree. Roger Morigi knew talent when he saw it, even if it did leave him speechless.

The Tempest Does Pass

Morigi admitted it. He did have a temper and it would flare up given the right provocation. And when provoked, Morigi's five-foot-three-inch, 125 pound frame suddenly took on the dimensions of a twelve-foot, two-ton behemoth. Typical of the Italian temperament, however, the temper would flash and then pass away.

He recalled one time when there were a number of stone carvers on the job and he would go around to the several work areas checking on their progress. He came upon several who had been on a coffee break that Morigi felt had lasted too long. The temper flashed.

"Maybe I should get a deck of cards for you and then you could have a nice game of bridge," he shouted.

The workers dispersed and sheepishly went back to work. But Morigi's anger was building. He took the workers' elevator down to the ground and as the elevator descended, his anger escalated. As he exited the elevator, he saw John Bayless, the Cathedral Business Manager and Curator, waiting for the lift. Still feeling the effect of his wrath, Morigi called out to his good friend Bayless, "And that goes for you too!"

Bayless was stunned. "Why don't you go to my office and sit down for a bit," he suggested.

"Sit down?" replied Morigi. "That's the trouble with this place now. There are too many people sitting down!"

The next morning, Morigi was hard at work carving when Bayless came by.

"Good morning," called Morigi. "It's a beautiful day!"

"Yes," responded Bayless. "It's always a beautiful day after the storm has passed."

Raking the Leaves

Before Richard Feller was appointed as Clerk of the Works, that function was performed by Canon G. Gardner Monks, a man whom Morigi described as educated as an engineer, but not as an art consultant.

Having grown up in Italy, Morigi learned early to appreciate the many adornments and embellishments of the cathedrals and public buildings. He was especially observant of the many stone carvings and the great variety of subject matter displayed in them.

When he first came to work at the cathedral, Canon Monks asked him to carve some capitals of columns and some of the minor bosses. When Morigi asked what subject matter he was to carve, Monks would always reply that he should carve some leaves.

After several weeks, he went to Monks one day and said he wanted to go to a hardware store and buy a rake.

"We have a rake in the tool shed," replied Monks.

"Yes, I know," said Morigi. "But one rake will never clean up all of these leaves you have me carving." The Canon got the message and from then on he would ask for suggestions, usually agreeing with recommendations made to him.

The Face of Real Beauty

One day when Morigi and his associate Edward Ratti were hard at work, an official of the cathedral came by with his wife whom he introduced to Morigi. When Morigi looked up and saw her, he said he almost shouted, for he had never seen an uglier woman in his life. She was so ugly he confesses that he tried not to look at her.

Then, says Morigi, he experienced an incident that he has never forgotten. "If I live to be a hundred, I'll never forget it. Never, never, never, will I forget that!"

She began talking to Morigi, asking him questions about his work, commenting on his carving, making observations about the cathedral's progress. After a few minutes, Morigi was suddenly impressed by how beautiful and lovely she was. The more she talked, the lovelier she became.

After the woman and her husband departed, Morigi and Ratti discussed the incident and they were both in agreement concerning their initial and subsequent impressions of her.

It is an interesting thought; one can only contrast this incident with those times when one has seen a very beautiful woman, only to note her beauty fade as soon as she began to speak. After all, real beauty is more than skin deep. It requires substance!

99

You Don't Question Genius

Morigi remembers one day when the late Fred Maynard, a construction superintendent for the George M. Fuller Company was walking through the construction yard in the company of Philip Hubert Frohman. As they walked by the huge stockpile of stones just received from the quarry in Indiana, Mr. Frohman pointed to one stone and said to Maynard, "That stone has been cut improperly. It will not fit."

Maynard was aghast! Every stone from the quarry was cut according to the exact dimensions that were specified in the cathedral plans. Further, a metal template had been sent to the finishing mill to be used as a pattern, to be sure that the right dimensions were observed. Finally, every stone was given a discreet serial number that was painted on the inside of the stone, so that the masons would always put the correct stone in the place intended for it. How could the architect look at the group of several hundred stones piled in the construction yard, and selecting one, pronounce it to be the improper dimensions?

"Don't ever question that man," counseled Morigi. "When you get to know him you will understand. Go check your drawings."

Maynard checked the serial number of the stone, looked at the ticket order for the stone and the template dimensions. Frohman was right. The stone was wrong. Maynard was amazed. Morigi smiled.

The Right Man in the Right Job

One of Morigi's responsibilities as the Master Carver, was to assign the other carvers to the many jobs that had to be accomplished. The carvers were not equally skilled and some were far more competent than the others. This would not be apparent to the layman but to a carver, it was all too well known.

Fortunately, the jobs to be accomplished were not equally difficult. Some required a far greater degree of dexterity and talent while others were relatively simple. This made it possible for Morigi to assign each carver to the job for which he was best suited.

Now there is nothing especially novel about this and all would agree that to follow this way of assigning carvers to the various jobs would be most rational. But leave it to Morigi to put a special twist on it. As he said, it would be a waste of a man's talent to put a highly skilled carver on simple jobs. But if he put a less skilled carver on a difficult job, it would take him much longer to complete the task, requiring the cathedral to pay out many more hours of labor. To Morigi, this was the same as stealing from the cathedral!

How many times has the cathedral, along with other employers, been required to pay the penalty when the employees contrived to expand the job to consume the time available for it.

The Cathedral Open House

For one of the annual Open House celebrations, the person in charge of the arrangements asked Morigi if he would set up a stone carving exhibit to demonstrate his art. He agreed even though he was unsure of how to proceed. After all, it takes years of hard work to master the skill and no one would be interested in standing and watching him carve a stone. "Perhaps," he thought, "it would be best to appeal to the children."

Morigi assembled several carved stones as exhibits of how finished stones appeared. Then he took one uncarved stone and explained to the children in the area that there was a finished carving trapped in the stone and that they must release it. He showed them how to hold the chisel and how to hit it with a mallet in order to make a piece of stone fly out. The children were fascinated and each wanted to take a turn. They stood patiently in line while a child would take his or her turn and when that child caused a piece of stone to fly off, Morigi would say, "All right, that was good. Now let's give the next person a chance."

But the line of children never diminished. As soon as a child finished a turn with the chisel and mallet, the child would go immediately to the end of the line in order to have another turn.

'Hands-on' experience is always more satisfying than merely watching a demonstration.

101

Roger Morigi carving the statue of St. Margaret of Scotland. The sculptor was W. M. McVey.

Photo by A.C. Barrett

John H. Bayless

He was born in Covington, Kentucky. His parents died when he was but a small lad and he was raised by two aunts in Meyersdale, Pennsylvania. He attended public schools in Pennsylvania and was certified a school teacher by California State College in California, Pennsylvania. He taught school for two years before he came to Washington. Teaching was not his choice; it had been a necessity. When he came to Washington, he attended the George Washington University, concentrating in economics and journalism.

In 1930 he was employed at Washington National Cathedral as an assistant to the Curator, becoming the Curator in 1935. In 1953, he also became the Business Manager of the Cathedral Foundation. In this position he had responsibility not only for the cathedral, but for the several schools on the close as well.

✚   Shortly after his employment at the cathedral, Bayless became fascinated with the subject of stained glass. He studied and acquired a very detailed knowledge of the subject. In the early years, Lawrence Saint, one of the cathedral's principal stained-glass artists maintained a fabrication studio in nearby Pennsylvania. Bayless spent a considerable amount of time with Mr. Saint and considered his education on stained glass to have been greatly enhanced by that association. Bayless built up a superb collection of slides on stained glass and developed a reputation as one of the foremost lay authorities on stained glass in the country.

✚   Bayless took over responsibility for the Christmas Card program at the cathedral. Jointly with his wife, they managed the program for many years enabling it to increase in size many times over. The program has continued to grow far more than anyone might have predicted. As Bayless admits with a smile, "We had the ideal relationship for a husband and wife team. She made the money and I spent it."

✦ In 1958, he and his wife Edna traveled as agents of the Cathedral Chapter to England, France, Spain, Germany, Italy, Holland and Belgium to study the glass in European cathedrals. This experience led him to make some changes in windows already installed at the cathedral and to change the stated policy for new windows to be fabricated. They also visited museums and art galleries to discover many new subjects for the cathedral Christmas Card series.

✦ Always active as a scout master with the Boy Scout program, his troop Number Five of St. Albans Church was the largest troop in Washington, numbering some 100 boys. During his 27 years with the scouting program, he had 92 scouts attain the Eagle rank. Bayless was awarded the Silver Beaver award, the highest honor that is given to a scout master.

✦ Bayless was one of the more avid bird watchers associated with the cathedral. An article in the *Cathedral Age* for Summer 1947 revealed that during the spring of that year, he had identified and classified 75 species on the cathedral close.

In the 1930s and 1940s, there was no office of visitor services at the cathedral as there is today. All visitors and tourists came through the office of the Curator. Bayless personally greeted many of the visitors, estimating as many as 250,000 each year and he lectured throughout the country on the iconography of the cathedral.

In those early days of the cathedral's construction, with the small number of staff employed, the luxury of specialization was not an alternative for consideration. People had to perform many different functions and Bayless certainly was prominent among them. As a licensed lay reader, he would read the prayer services at noon or at Evensong in the absence of a priest. He wrote a number of articles for the *Cathedral Age* and served as an assistant editor. On occasion, he taught classes at the St. Albans School for Boys, and during the World War II years, he was a full member of the faculty. Determined to make the cathedral's funds go as far as possible, he set up a joint arrangement with the American University and Georgetown University Hospital so that the three institutions purchased their supplies together, saving significant funds for each.

Retiring from the cathedral in 1976, Bayless sold real estate in the Washington area for ten years. He and his wife Edna now reside in Wilson, North Carolina.

Making the Stained Glass Brighter

In the early days of the cathedral construction, artists were forbidden to use silver-white glass in the fabrication of stained-glass windows. They were encouraged to use only the primary, and more vivid colors so that a greater display of color would be apparent to the viewer inside the building. As a result, many of the windows were quite dark.

On his trip to Europe, Bayless was able to climb scaffolding to many of the windows in the European cathedrals, and in doing so he discovered that a quantity of silver-white glass had been used in the 13th-century windows. The result was very pleasing, admitting more light to the building and providing a better contrast for the vivid colors also contained in the windows.

He also discovered how to apply hydrofluoric acid to selected spots in installed windows to add highlights to portions of the glass that appeared too dark at floor level. Standing on the floor with a walkie-talkie radio, he could communicate with artists at the window level who would apply the acid and then neutralize it in order to obtain the proper effect. One of the artists, Joseph Reynolds, who created the south rose window, referred to the process as "tuning the window," much as one might tune an organ.

After his return from the visit to Europe, and the results of his initial "tuning" of the windows were viewed, he served as chairman of a committee that revised the policy on the use of silver-white glass in the cathedral.

The Ashes in the Ambry

During the early days of construction at the cathedral, in the 1920s, a stone mason went to Bishop Harding with a very unusual request. According to the mason, his wife had always been unusually proud of the fact that her husband worked at Mt. St. Albans and that he was helping to build a cathedral. It was one of the foremost joys in her life that he went each day to that wonderful and elevated position. Now, his wife had died and he would like to have her buried at the cathedral.

Bishop Harding was thoughtful and extended his sympathy to the mason in his bereavement, but he was not able to grant the request. He explained that the Cathedral Chapter had established very rigid rules concerning who could be interred at the cathedral and he was unable to grant any exception to that policy. The mason was disappointed but he understood.

Following that incident, a story circulated that the mason had arranged for his wife's body to be cremated and that he had then mixed the ashes with mortar, assuring that his wife would, in fact, be interred in the cathedral's fabric. But it was just a story. It had never been documented and it was assumed that the story was a fabrication, another of the legends, the folklore, that grow up around the construction of cathedrals.

Somewhat later, in 1941, it became necessary to provide an expanded and enlarged area for the Books of Remembrance, the listings of those for whom gifts are given. The books had been kept in the Ambry, a niche in one of the piers in the chancel. The number of books had increased to such an extent that one of the stone carvers, Italo Fanfani, was asked to enlarge the niche.

Fanfani worked with his chisels and hammers and made real progress in enlarging the opening, when suddenly the resistance of the stone was gone. There was a void behind the stone. Investigating, he found a small deposit of ashes. Bayless, who was standing beside Fanfani at the time, was astonished. There had never been anything like this uncovered at the cathedral before. Was it really ashes from a cremation? Was it the cremated remains of the mason's wife? There was no way of knowing, of course, but one had to assume that it was the cremated remains of a human. And if it were the remains of a human being then it should not be interred formally, unless a name could be assigned to it.

Italo Fanfani's son Jack, later a stone carver in his own right, and Assistant Clerk of the Works, has a vivid recollection of the incident. He recalls the discussion of the event in his home and the serious concern his parents expressed about the incident.

The ashes were preserved in a small envelope that was re-interred between two stones in a portion of the cathedral being constructed at that time. Only the senior Fanfani knew where. There may be another person interred at the cathedral other than those appearing on the official list maintained in the archives. Only God knows who it might be, but that is all that matters.

The Carving of Ishmael

On frequent occasions, Bayless would climb scaffolding to inspect the progress of the stone carvers at work, transforming plain stones to works of art. He had a special relationship with Roger Morigi, the Master Carver, and he greatly enjoyed visiting with Morigi, even though he never could guess what Morigi might say or do in any given circumstance. If there was one thing predictable about Morigi, it was that he was always unpredictable. Perhaps this was one of the things most fascinating to Bayless.

It was in the 1960s and Morigi was working on the label molds of Bay Six, nave north aisle. One particular carving featured Hagar, the Egyptian maid to Sarah, with her son Ishmael, the son of Abraham. After Hagar and Ishmael had been banished from Sarah's tent, they traveled to the wilderness of Beer-sheba. Morigi was carving a full relief of Hagar giving water to Ishmael while he was seated under a palm tree. Bayless was fascinated with the great detail that Morigi was carving in the palm leaves.

"Why are you carving such detail in those leaves?" he asked. "They are a good 25 feet above the floor and no one will ever see that detail."

"God knows its there," replied Morigi.

How can one argue with that? So often Morigi's response would leave no room for any reply. Bayless descended the ladder and left Morigi with his carving.

Cathedral Roof Slide

Youth has the ability to be absolutely incorrigible and impossible to comprehend. The typical youth assumes that nothing he undertakes to do will ever cause any danger for him and that he is, essentially, immortal. And, of course, to embrace such a belief will allow a young man to do just about anything that comes to his mind and the more awe inspiring it is, the better. If it frightens others, that's all right, because nothing adverse is going to happen to him.

When the new roof was installed on the cathedral's north transept, it was a most tempting target for two young men. The sheets of lead are put together with crimped folds that protrude about one inch, making one inch high ridges all the way from the parapet up to the peak of the roof. By wearing rubber sole sneakers, and using the ridges one can pull oneself all the way up to the top of the roof and then encounter a most exhilarating slide down to the bottom.

Bayless was called one day by the cathedral guards because two young men had converted the new roof to a sliding board and were having a hilarious time, causing a woman watching to faint because she did not know that there was a parapet at the bottom of the roof to catch the boys and prevent their sliding into space.

The most interesting thing about this incident was the way that Bayless disciplined the two boys. Rather than sending them packing, he took the two boys aside and counseled them, challenged them and encouraged them. They became active in the Boy Scout program and in time, both became Eagle Scouts. Bayless followed them into their later lives, one in the Army, the other in the Navy. Both had distinguished careers.

Patience is usually preferable to petulance.

Walter Lippman and the Bells

The first Dean of Washington National Cathedral was the Reverend Dr. George C. F. Bratenahl. He and his wife, Mrs. Florence Bratenahl built a home in 1917 on Woodley Road at the corner of 36th Street. A very commodious residence, the house remained in the family until 1945 when it was sold to the well known columnist, Walter Lippmann. Lippmann and his wife lived in the house for 22 years.

Probably one of the most influential columnists of this century, Lippmann helped found *The New Republic* in 1914 and served for some years as its assistant editor. During World War I, he was an assistant to Secretary of War Newton D. Baker. After the armistice, he was selected to go to France to participate in the negotiations for the Treaty of Versailles. His writings are said to have greatly influenced President Wilson who drew on many of Lippmann's ideas for his settlement plan and for the League of Nations.

Lippmann's intellectual contributions continued after he moved to his new home across from the cathedral. It served not only as his residence, but also as his office, and it was from that location that he wrote his column "Today and Tomorrow" for the *New York Herald Tribune* that was in turn syndicated to some 250 other newspapers in the United States and abroad. It was a perfect location. He lived near to the seat of power in the United States that provided very privileged sources of information, yet his office faced the quiet, almost bucolic setting of the cathedral close, a beautiful vista that could not fail to provide the environment for the birth of great ideas. How fortunate he was!

In 1963, while the central tower was being constructed, the ten peal bells and the 53 carillon bells arrived from the foundries in England and were installed. Here was something new and the bell ringers selected to ring the many peals felt compelled to practice for hours to establish their expertise. It seemed that those bells rang morning, noon and night. They drove Lippmann to distraction. In one of his columns he wrote, "I can't think, for those damned cathedral bells!"

The Bratenahl House.
At one time, the residence of the Walter Lippmans, now the residence of the Cathedral Dean.

Peace was destroyed.

To avoid an incident that could have had international repercussions, Dean Sayre ordered insulation installed on the inside of the north and west tower louvers and wooden mutes fastened to the bell clappers during practice sessions so that the bells were barely audible at ground level.

Peace was restored.

In 1967, when Lippmann moved back to New York, he sold the house to the Cathedral Foundation. Bayless conducted the negotiations and handled the purchase for the cathedral. When Lippman departed, Bayless took one of the dozen small commemorative bells that had come with the large ones from England, wrapped it as a gift and presented it to Lippmann. The significance of the gift was apparent. Much amused, Lippmann kept the small bell on his desk in New York.

Peace was preserved!

The Bells Can Ring the Boys

When the bell peal was installed, it became a source of fascination for many of the younger boys who wanted to become trained bell ringers. The peals are extremely complicated and it takes great concentration on the part of those who participate. Because of the al-

107

most infinite number of combinations and sequences in ringing, some of the peals require hours to complete. In addition, the youngsters need to learn safety procedures early and to appreciate the need to observe them at all times.

The ten bells are located on a floor in the central tower with ropes used to ring them extended through ten holes in the floor, one for each bell, to the floor below. The holes in the upper floor measure only about two inches in diameter, very small holes, but sufficiently large to allow the ropes to pass through without binding.

One of the principal surprises for new ringers is the weight of the bells and the great pull the bells exert on the ropes as they tumble to and fro. Ringers are cautioned not to wrap the rope around their hands or wrists since a bell can lift one off the floor as the rope is pulled back through the hole by the bell above.

On one occasion, an instructor was teaching a new group how to participate in a ring and the trainees, who were very young lads, were eager to achieve full competence as soon as possible. One of the boys was so intent on certain facets of the operation, he failed to notice that the rope had become tangled around his wrist so that when the bell tumbled above, the lad was pulled up almost to the ceiling. The young boy was terrified and all of the other ringers were also frightened, releasing their ropes almost as if they were too hot to hold. The instructor disengaged the rope from the young boy's wrist and then, pointing to the small two inch holes in the ceiling, said, "So far, I have never lost a boy through one of those holes."The tension was relaxed. The boys could smile. But a valuable lesson had been learned.

The Bayless Peppermint Snake

Water appeared in some of the burial vaults in portions of the crypt that signified a leak somewhere in the cathedral. Water can be the most insidious of substances. From where could it have come?

An exhaustive survey of the roof drainage and run-off of surface water seemed to establish that the water was coming from another source. There was suspicion that it might even be from the heating system in the floor of the nave. In order to provide heat for something as large as the cathedral, pipe had been laid under the marble floor and connected to a hot water heating system in the Central Heating Plant. Hot water pumped through this maze provided a very pleasant convection heating in the building. But the necessity of taking up some two acres of the marble floor to find one leak, and thereby risk damaging other portions of the piping, was not an option that appealed to Bayless. The cost alone would be prohibitive.

First he had to be sure that the water was coming from the heating system. He had the engineers in the heating plant add a quantity of peppermint extract to the hot water and when the odor of peppermint became strong in the crypt, then he knew he had located the source of the water.

Two friends in the Bureau of Standards told Bayless of the success a firm in nearby Maryland had experienced using a thermograph to solve such a problem. He called a Mr. S. T. Dunn of Silver Spring to the cathedral with his thermography equipment to run a test. The equipment had a scope, similar to a computer monitor, and temperature changes under the marble floor would appear on the scope that could trace the piping wherever it went.

The heating plant was closed down so that all water in the floor of the cathedral would cool. When it was re-started, the thermograph was able to trace the hot water through the pipes showing a veritable snake on the scope of the machine. Finally the scope showed a large dispersal of water under the floor and they knew then and there that the source of the problem had been discovered.

When the floor was removed, it was found that the concrete poured at that particular portion of the nave had been treated with salt. It had been poured in cold weather and the salt was used to prevent the concrete from freezing. However, it was used against the specifications that had been issued by the builders. There was to be no salt in the concrete because the pipe was to be laid next to it. One could be certain that with the passage of years some water would seep through the marble floor when it was being cleaned, and when water combined with salt in the concrete, the chemical reaction created a weak hydrochloric acid that was less than compatible with the metal pipe. When the concrete was replaced and the pipe repaired, the issue was resolved.

The method of solving this problem appealed to the press and a story appeared in one of the local publications entitled "The Bayless Peppermint Snake." It is certainly a strange subject to be associated with constructing a cathedral, but then ingenuity will always invite the unusual.

The Unique Woodcarving

When Bayless retired from the cathedral in 1976, he became active in real estate. He had received a significant amount of experience in managing the cathedral's properties and he was also a person of unusual energy. It was to be expected that within a year he would be found at the top of the 1500 real estate agents in his new company.

On one occasion he went to a neighborhood house in the community to make an appraisal and he noticed a very beautiful piece of woodcarving. He examined it and remarked to the woman who resided in the house, that it was an excellent example of real craftsmanship, saying that he knew of only one person capable of the quality shown in the woodcarving, Ernest Pelligrini of Boston.

"That is very interesting," the woman responded. "He was my father."

The two of them laughed and made the usual comment that follows such an incident about living in a small world.

When he had completed the appraisal and was ready to leave

the house, Bayless returned again to the woodcarving and asked if he could bring a friend to see it. "He is the Master Stone Carver at the cathedral, his name is Roger Morigi."

"Roger Morigi?" the woman responded. "Why he and I came from the same village in Italy, and as young people we used to go together many years ago!"

The small world syndrome intensified!

The Administration Building Was Born in the Hospital

John Bayless had gone to the hospital for surgery but he did not intend to release all of his responsibilities while he was there. There are some people who seem to enjoy poor health, or at least, to enjoy talking about it. Others do not know how to enjoy the privilege of being sick. Bayless was one of the latter.

It had been planned that an administration building should be built for the staff at the cathedral and that it should be joined to the cathedral by cloisters at the northeast. While recuperating from his surgery, Bayless obtained a board that he could place over his knees to serve as something of a table and allow him to draw sketches.

The Northeast Cloisters and the Administration Building.

Photo by Stewart Brothers

Since he had studied mechanical drawing, he was able to draw floor plans to serve as the preliminary plans for the present Administration Building at the cathedral.

The building was constructed of concrete blocks and then painted white. It was a modest facility, and modesty would always become any administrative activity, no matter what the organization. In time, the building acquired the name of *That Whited Wall*, a somewhat adolescent cognomen, yet most descriptive.

In later years, Mr. Philip Frohman, the cathedral architect, designed an additional floor for the building and the entire facility was encased in limestone. Shorn of its initial modesty, the building now resembles nothing so much as a middle-aged dowager, who knows her importance to the social scene and is determined to fulfill that obligation. We should remember, however, that the building had a most modest beginning, on the knees of a sick man in the hospital.

Reaching Out

During World War II, Bayless served on the Board of Directors of the Pastoral Institute. He did not tell this story; but the source is unimpeachable. It serves to distinguish the character of the man.

Bayless heard on the radio of a man in southern Maryland, the father of several children, whose small home had burned to the ground. The welfare people acting in what they perceived to be the best interests of the family, planned to find homes for the children, splitting up the family.

This was not acceptable to Bayless. From Philip Frohman he obtained detailed architectural drawings for a small house. He recruited carpenters, plumbers, and electricians from the cathedral community. He obtained gifts of building materials from labor unions and other individuals. He persuaded the unions to allow the members to donate their time without compensation. He obtained the services of a number of boy scouts from the troop of which he was master.

The following week, the family in southern Maryland received a new home and were able to stay together. With his small army of volunteers, Bayless practiced the kind of outreach that touches people most directly. Unlike so many of us, he did not wait for someone else to initiate action. He always was a self-starter.

A Murder at the Cathedral

Margaret Truman Daniel wrote a book some years ago on this subject. Although it was highly entertaining, her work was all fictional. Change the setting, the victim, the murder weapon and the felon and the work is no longer fantasy.

A woman employed as the librarian at the cathedral had been irritated repeatedly by one of the janitors on the close who was assigned to cleaning the library. He did not clean as thoroughly as she believed he should and she reproached him about doing a very poor job. On occasion she would place scraps of trash at places in the building to see if he would find them and remove them. This so irritated the janitor that the relationship between the two of them developed into a vendetta.

One morning early, Bayless received a call at home from the librarian's mother who was distraught. She told Bayless that her daughter had not returned home the previous evening and she was worried. When he arrived at the cathedral, Bayless went at once to the Library. As soon as he saw the librarian's sweater folded on a chair at her desk and her purse next to it, Bayless became concerned. He searched the building until he found the lifeless body of the woman dumped into a utility access area below the building. She had been killed by a blow from a heavy piece of wood. In the trial that followed, the janitor was found guilty and executed. He was the last person to be so executed in the District of Columbia.

This was an incident that many associated with the cathedral would prefer to forget and certainly not to include with a book of this nature. But as unpleasant as it is, the incident serves to remind us that both saints and sinners can be employed at the cathedral where the staff ministers to "all sorts and conditions of men."

They Held the Cathedral Hostage

John Bayless awarded a contract to build a swimming pool at the Beauvoir School. The pool had been designed by a well known architectural firm and the construction contract was awarded to a good firm, well known in the area as a builder. But the construction firm was over extended and went bankrupt. That caused quite a few headaches for Bayless although he eventually got the pool completed and in service. He thought the matter was finished. But one of the strange facets of administration assures us that although we may take our rest when we believe we are through, the opposition is still alert, alive and awaiting an opportunity to pounce.

And pounce they did!

There was another contracting action that Bayless planned to take that was completely unrelated to the swimming pool. He wanted to have steam lines placed under Woodley Road that would provide heat from the cathedral heating plant to one of the buildings for the National Cathedral School for Girls. In order to have this contract awarded, he needed a building permit from the District of Columbia. But the permit was denied. It seemed that some of the sub-contractors had not been paid by the contractor who had the swimming pool project, so they had a lien placed on the Washington National Cathedral until they were paid. But the cathedral had paid its money to the contractor. The cathedral was being held hostage!

Bayless eventually resolved the problem but he had learned a lesson. He had the cathedral close divided into a number of plats on the District of Columbia land records so that an action in the future against one part of the close would not affect the total area.

For Action, Go to the Top

The cathedral wanted to obtain the services of Patrick Plunkett. He was a skilled and reputable stone carver, an Englishman who wished to work at the Washington Cathedral. But each time an application was made to the Immigration Service, it had been refused. There were sufficient stone carvers in the United States, they said, and there was no need to import any more.

Bayless investigated. The Immigration Service considered anyone who performed any type of service with cutting or excising stone to be a stone carver. Thus persons cutting letters in grave stones were considered to be in the same category with the artists who transformed the intricacies of plaster sculpture to a finished statue. The difference was explained but still the request was refused.

Bayless was frustrated that he had been unable to explain the difference and to clarify for the authorities the need that was becoming more and more critical. In his frustration one day, he picked up the telephone at noon and called the regional office in Philadelphia. The telephone rang for an extended period, most of the office members had gone to lunch. Finally, the call was answered by the Commissioner himself. Bayless explained his predicament to sympathetic ears and the problem was resolved. Patrick Plunkett joined the cathedral stone carvers where he worked for many years, contributing countless numbers of carvings for the finished cathedral.

And it all happened because Bayless happened to telephone when all of the Immigration staff had gone to lunch.

Bishop Freeman, the Economist

Bishop James E. Freeman was known to be a great preacher. When it was announced that he would preach, the cathedral would be filled to overflowing. He was a study in contrasts as well. He frequently wore a cape in inclement weather. It seemed to fly out horizontally behind him, trying to catch up as he ran over the cathedral grounds, a choreograph of flying arms and legs, each moving more rapidly than the other. He was described as "an earthly manifestation of God in the guise of Ichabod Crane!"

Bishop Freeman had studied economics in his earlier years and he would remark frequently that he could match wits with any economist. He often commented on fiscal programs of the federal government in either positive or negative terms and he was never hesitant to express his opinions.

When the National Recovery Act was being considered and debated by Congress in the early 1930s, Bishop Freeman requested he be called to testify, and he gave the proposed Act very low marks. It was his judgment that the Act would impose undue hardship on the country, that it should not be approved and that it should be defeated. President Franklin Roosevelt took due notice of this opposition but kept his counsel.

It was some time later when the King and Queen of Great Britain were visiting the United States, the President escorted them around Washington to see some of the more interesting sights in the city. One of the scheduled stops was to be the Washington Cathedral, which by that time consisted of only the apse, choir and north transept. Bishop Freeman donned his finest clerical garb including his miter, and stood ready with his staff to receive the visitors at the designated entrance. As the cars came to the entrance, the President is alleged to have said that his Royal Visitors had seen many finished cathedrals in Great Britain, they could not possibly be interested in the mere beginning of one in this country. They drove by. Bishop Freeman was left to regret that his visitors did not come in.

It was generally agreed among members of the cathedral staff, that it was not the status of construction at the cathedral that deterred the visitors; it was the counsel previously given on the National Recovery Act.

Labor or Management

When Jack Fanfani first came to the cathedral as a stone carver, he had worked at this position for only a year or so when he was elected president of the Washington Stone Cutters and Carvers Labor Union. This was appropriate. He was a personable individual, he was a good carver, he also had management skills. He served well as the union president.

Shortly after his election, Fanfani was assigned to the Clerk of the Works office at the cathedral as an assistant to Richard Feller. In this position, he had supervisory responsibilities over many of the stone carvers. Now that he was in a management position, he would be expected to relinquish his position as president of the local union. But that did not happen. Fanfani was re-elected as president even though he was now in management. That was the way the union members wanted it.

It was fortunate for the cathedral that a labor problem did not arise during Fanfani's tenure as both Assistant Clerk of the Works and also president of the Stone Cutters and Carvers Union. He would certainly have had real difficulty in negotiating with himself.

Every Problem Has an Answer

Bayless was sitting in his office one day when one of the secretaries in the Administration Building came to see him about a family problem. It was very obvious that she was distraught; it was difficult for her to hold back her tears.

A new mother and Roman Catholic in her belief, she had traveled to St. Louis with her husband and new baby, to have the child baptized in her childhood parish. Because she and her husband had not been married in the Catholic Church, however, she was refused the sacrament of baptism for her child. She wanted very much to have her child baptized and to be raised in her church. Bayless thought he saw a solution.

Over the years, administrators at the cathedral had come into contact with many clergy from different denominations and faiths. Bayless had become a close friend to a Roman Catholic priest who was in charge of many of the parochial schools in the Washington area. He explained the problem to the priest who came to the cathedral and baptized the baby in the Children's Chapel in a private ceremony. The certificate of baptism was then registered at one of the Roman Catholic parishes in Washington.

For every rule that men create, there can be a manmade solution if we only search for it.

Eight Heads on a Buttress

It is not the title of a song. Perhaps you are thinking of "Four Coins in the Fountain." But it is a very real event that has been preserved in stone for posterity.

It was in 1960, during the last phases of constructing the south transept, that eight persons who had given so much of themselves to the cathedral, were honored in a special ceremony. On the top facing stones, of the first pinnacle supported by a buttress on the west side of the south transept, eight heads have been carved rather than the crockets that typically decorate the stones at that location.

The eight heads are of:

- ✚ PHILIP HUBERT FROHMAN, *Principal Cathedral Architect*
- ✚ CARL L. BUSH, *one of the principal sculptors*
- ✚ JOHN H. BAYLESS, *Curator and Business Manager*
- ✚ BENJAMIN THORON, *former Business Manager and Foundation Treasurer*
- ✚ PAUL CALLAWAY, *Third Cathedral Organist and Choirmaster*
- ✚ RICHARD WAYNE DIRKSEN, *Fourth Cathedral Organist and Choirmaster*
- ✚ DEAN FRANCIS B. SAYRE, JR. *Cathedral Dean from 1951 to 1978*
- ✚ CANON LUTHER D. MILLER, *Canon Precentor*

L to R:
Philip H. Frohman, Carl Bush,
John Bayless, Benjamin Thoron.

Photo by Brooks Photographers

L to R:
Paul Callaway, Richard Wayne Dirksen,
Dean Sayre, Canon Luther Miller.

Photo by Brooks Photographers

Richard Feller called on Constantine Seferlis to model the likenesses of the eight persons being honored. Being a skilled sculptor as well as a stone carver, Seferlis had no difficulty with this assignment except for the likeness of Thoron. Lacking photographs of Thoron that he could use, he went to Thoron's office several times and stood at the door looking in to study his features. On one occasion, Thoron called out to Seferlis asking if he could help him with anything. Seferlis could not disclose anything concerning his assignment and said he needed no help. Thoron was heard to mutter, "Someone ought to give that Greek a job!"

All eight men were richly deserving of the accolades given them. It is altogether appropriate that their likenesses should be preserved in "high places."

Two Bees in a Boss

As mentioned in the introduction to this section, John Bayless retired from the cathedral in 1975. At that time, his friends gave very generously for embellishments in the cathedral fabric to commemorate his service. As the construction of the west towers progressed, a dedication of these gifts occurred at the Evensong on October 12, 1983. On that occasion, Bishop John Walker presided and accepted the gifts on behalf of the cathedral.

The first gift was a stained-glass window in the northwest turret stairs rising from the northwest porch. Designed and fabricated by Henry Lee Willet, a well known American glass designer and long-time friend of Bayless, it is a collage of symbols in a mosaic of glass that represents some of Bayless' many interests. A fish, the most ancient Christian symbol, dominates the design. It is also representative of Bayless' love of fly casting. A cogged wheel represents his long association with Rotary International and a silver beaver, the scouting award given to him. A carrier pigeon with an envelope is symbolic of the long tenure both Bayless and his wife Edna had with the cathedral Christmas Card department. And, of course, the stained-glass window itself, that is representative of his significant contribution to the cathedral windows.

The second gift was the center keystone boss in the north nave aisle gallery that was the creative expression of Constantine Seferlis, a sculptor/carver who has long been associated with the cathedral. Carved *in situ*, the foliage in the center is a "Della Robbia Wreath" surrounded by scenes of the Nativity. In addition to Mary and Joseph with the infant Jesus, there are shepherds with their sheep, a Christmas tree and the Magi.

It would probably never be noticed by the average observer, but stone carvers are given full latitude to express themselves in their work and Seferlis did so in his "Della Robbia Wreath." If one looks closely he can see two bees carved on the foliage, one for John and one for Edna, long known to cathedral staff as "Mr. and Mrs. B." Seferlis did not differentiate between them, but anyone who knows the two would agree that it is not necessary to do so.

117

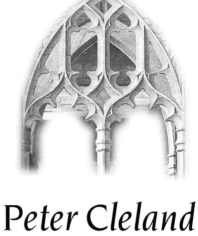

Peter Cleland

Peter Cleland's parents immigrated from Scotland to Cleveland, Ohio in 1920. A year later, young Peter was born, who like his father and brother, was destined to become a stone mason. The name Peter is not well known in Washington; mention Billy Cleland and there is instant recognition.

Billy graduated from high school in Wilkinsburg, Pennsylvania and then began his apprenticeship as a mason in Washington, D.C. in 1941. In just one year he was in the Navy where he served until 1945.

After leaving the Navy, Billy worked in Washington at many different projects demonstrating his ability as a stone mason and accruing a number of distinguished credits to his record.

+ Construction of the National Gallery of Art
+ Construction of the Jefferson Memorial
+ Renovation of the White House
+ Renovation of the Dirksen Senate Office Building
+ Construction of the Sam Rayburn House Office Building
+ Supervised the stone construction of the Kennedy grave site

In January 1972, Billy came to the Washington National Cathedral as the cathedral's Master Mason where he remained until his retirement in 1989 and the construction of the cathedral nearing completion. Although his sons elected not to follow the stone setting tradition of the Clelands, Billy had the rare opportunity of seeing two of his grandsons working as masons in the final construction days at the cathedral. He was re-called from retirement on September 30, 1990 to send up the final stone to be set in the cathedral's fabric.

Billy and his wife Altha live in Clinton, Maryland. Serving as a member of the Preservation Committee, Billy still journeys to the cathedral periodically when one may be certain to hear a good story as well as some very practical advice on preserving the stone surface at the cathedral.

A Young Mason's Education

Billy Cleland has never been able to get away from the memory of Alec Ewan. Ewan had immigrated to the United States from Scotland and he became a very close friend of Billy's father. After all, he was Scottish too.

Ewan came to know Billy and in many respects regarded him almost as a grandson. It was because of Ewan that Billy's father had become a stone mason. Billy followed his father into the stone business and after World War II he began working at buildings in the Washington area. In the course of several years, Ewan became the Master Mason at the cathedral and since Billy had shown promise as a mason, Ewan employed him.

Shortly after Billy began working at the cathedral, Ewan asked him to set some stones on the south balcony and, Billy thought, he was a great deal more detailed in his instructions than was necessary. He suggested to Billy the way he should proceed and which stones he should set first. As Billy relates the story, "I was a young squirt and I thought I knew enough that I did not need any guidance from Ewan. I knew what was required and I knew how to do it."

Accordingly, Billy set the stones the way he thought they should be set, not the way that Ewan had suggested; and he had not completed too much of the job before he got into trouble and had to call for Ewan. "When he came back, his nose was almost touching mine as he expressed his opinion of me and in the course of doing so, he proceeded to enlarge my vocabulary significantly."

During the next few years, one of the stone carvers carved Ewan's likeness on a post in the south balcony, looking directly at the wall where Billy had had his trouble. No matter where he stood, Billy could still see that face and remember the liberal education he received.

A Safety Record

Nothing gives Cleland greater satisfaction than the safety record he achieved as Master Mason at the cathedral. Having had considerable experience as a mason, he knew first hand the kinds of trouble one could encounter and the opportunities for disaster that faced a

119

Carving of Master Mason Alec Ewan.

mason daily. There was no job undertaken in which he did not review with the masons those precautions that should be observed to assure safety on the job. Further, each Monday morning, he met with the construction crews, masons and mason helpers, and he always covered some new or different angle of safety on the job.

During his years as Master Mason, *there was no significant accident involving a member of the construction crew.* There were the usual skinned knuckles and bruised shins, but no major accident. Cleland will tell you about this with an apparent sense of pride. He was concerned with his workers' safety and he considered it his responsibility.

The Cub Scout Master

One of the principal forms of entertainment for both workers and volunteers at the cathedral is to listen to the wonderful imagination and inventions of tour guides. It is always amazing that so much fantasy that is pure fiction is disclosed as fact; it is even more astounding that the public hearing it is ready to accept and believe.

Every stone that went into the cathedral's facade, was cut at the quarry to specifications determined by the architect, and a serial number was then affixed to the rear of the stone that disclosed where it was to be installed. As the stones arrived, they were placed in front of the cathedral under the grove of oak trees where they could be easily picked up on a dolly and taken to the hoist that would lift them into place to be set by a mason. In order to conserve space, the stones were grouped in the yard, placed in rows, and in sequence. They were geometric, they were neat, they had to be noticed.

Cleland was fascinated one day to hear a scout master standing amid the stones instructing his cub pack.

"This is the cathedral's graveyard," he told them. "It is quite old and you see that the tombstones are very close together. Years ago, people weren't as big as they are now. In fact they were very small so they could be buried in very small graves."

At this point Cleland was so convulsed that he missed the rest of the scout master's discourse.

Keeping up with Canon Martin

The Reverend Canon Charles Martin is almost as much a tradition at the cathedral as the cathedral itself. He served as the Headmaster at St. Alban's School for 28 years, to be followed by service as a canon at the cathedral. He was a familiar figure with his faithful bull dog walking around the cathedral he loved and looking into every facet of its construction and operation.

In his capacity as Master Mason, Bill Cleland was constantly checking on the activity of his masons and workmen. On one occasion, a swinging scaffold was being operated on the east end of the cathedral where masons were inspecting and pointing the mortar joints in some of the buttresses. When Cleland arrived, Canon Martin was standing watching the activity of the workmen high above the ground.

"I'll bet that would be great fun to take a ride on that scaffold," said the Canon.

Cleland demurred explaining to the Canon that safety requirements as well as insurance regulations made it mandatory that no one other than designated workmen were to ride on the scaffold. Canon Martin said nothing, however the twinkle in his eyes told Cleland that he had not been convincing and that he should watch the Canon carefully.

It was less than 24 hours later that Canon Martin saw Cleland and informed him how much he had enjoyed riding on the swinging scaffold! It should not have been surprising. Having been well educated by the boys at St. Albans for 28 years, the Canon knew all of the tricks.

Building a Rose Window

By the time the masons were ready to start building the tracery that constituted the great west rose window, Cleland realized he faced a dilemma. He had not been with the cathedral when the other two rose windows had been constructed, and none of the other masons had ever built a rose window. He knew that it would be essential for all measurements to be precise and all would need to be made from the same original point. He could not be certain that for something so massive the masons would always measure accurately and from the same point. He had to provide a reference that would be made available for all measurements.

A *mason setting the tracery stones in a cathedral window.*
Cathedral Archives

He had his carpenter and masons install angle irons across the opening, to form four 90-degree segments. These irons were affixed to the stone masonry of the west front wall so that they were rigid. He then acquired a five-eighths-inch bronze rod that he fitted to the angle irons so that it bisected the exact center of the proposed window, and that would be perpendicular to the plane of the angle irons. He acquired two steel tapes, fixing them to the ends of the bronze rod, one on the inside, the other on the outside of the window plane, so that masons could measure from either side but always measure from the same point and obtain the same identical reading.

This is not the kind of solution to a problem that is taught to masons. It is the kind of solution that imagination and ingenuity can devise. Fortunately, both conditions were not in short supply.

The Bells are Warranted

Some years after the bells had been installed in the central tower, a gentleman from the John Taylor Bell Foundry in Loughborough, England visited the cathedral. The gentleman, whose name has been lost with the passage of time, was on a holiday to America, and since the Taylor Foundry had manufactured all 53 bells for the cathedral's carillon he had been asked to stop by to see that all of the bells were functioning properly.

Master Mason Bill Cleland happened to be in the tower at that moment and was introduced to the visitor. This furnished the opportunity for some good natured banter between the two.

Cleland asked the visitor how long the Taylor Foundry had been casting bells and the visitor responded that the company had been in the bell business for several centuries.

"As a matter of fact," he volunteered, "We made the Liberty Bell in Philadelphia."

Cleland seized the opportunity. "Oh, so that's the kind of work you do. You know the Liberty Bell has been cracked for over two hundred years."

The visitor was not to be outdone. "Our company stands behind our work and warrants all of the bells we produce. We have told the United States, return the Liberty Bell in its original factory carton and we shall be happy to replace it."

A Sense of Humor

If there was one thing consistent about Billy Cleland, it was his sense of humor. It never left him. Billy loved a good story:

✦ Every Monday morning, all of the construction crew would gather outside of the Construction Office where Billy would share with them the plans and schedules for the week, ending always with another exhortation to safety. Once, after he had taken his family to visit Disney World in Florida, he appeared at the regular Monday meeting wearing an especially serious expression—and a large set of Mickey Mouse ears.

✚ Frequently, Billy was called on to give a slide presentation to an audience and to explain the process of building a cathedral. On one such occasion, he came to a slide that showed rows of stones in the construction yard waiting to be set in place. He explained that each stone had an alpha-numerical designation that indicated the precise place in the construction the stone was to be placed. He suddenly interrupted his presentation, walked up to the screen to look more closely at the picture and exclaimed, "Well, I'll be darned. I've been looking for that stone for the last month!"

✚ At the conclusion of the construction of the west front, it was necessary to convert the construction yard to a pedestrian court yard. Since the Construction Office was in the center of this area, the Construction Committee was quite concerned as to its disposition. Billy shocked the committee members by telling them that the Office building had been designated an historical landmark and that a bronze plaque would be placed on it the following week.

✚ After the Construction Committee members recovered from Cleland's ruse about the Construction Office, the Committee decided to have the building demolished with the debris carted away; it would be the least expensive way to dispose of the facility. A bulldozer proceeded to push the building over and then demolished the large panels so that there was just a giant pile of trash left. Billy stood in front of the pile and asked,"Did I slam the door too hard?"

The Telephone 'Ex-change'

By sometime during the 1980s the cathedral administrative family had outgrown its old telephone system. A completely new and enlarged system had to be installed to take care of the larger demands.

In the new system, new extension numbers were assigned that were different from previous numbers. As a matter of fact, the Construction Office was assigned a new extension identical to the previous extension assigned to the Cathedral Choral Society. As a result, Billy began receiving a number of calls that he had to direct to the Choral Society.

The new number did not cause any disruption in Billy's work but it did give him the opportunity to banter with Marion Leach, the Concert Manager of the Choral Society; and Billy would not allow such an opportunity to escape him. Meeting Ms. Leach on the close on day, he greeted her and added, "Oh, by the way, I have been directing calls for the Choral Society to your new number. But there have been so many of them that it just got out of hand. I have sent you a copy of a letter stating that I agreed to a concert for the Society a week from Saturday at a single's bar in Georgetown.

The Tuckers Two

This is the only section of this volume that features the memories of two persons. But it is not possible to separate the Tuckers; why should we wish to?

Lyn and Carl spent 28 years at the cathedral. In many respects, it was a fairy tale that came true. Carl was a flutist with the Birmingham Symphony at the time the tale begins. On Easter Sunday 1954, the two of them were house-bound with a "bug." They watched the Easter service from the Washington National Cathedral on television and Lyn remarked to Carl, "When you are in the National Symphony Orchestra and we live in Washington, we'll go to the cathedral every Sunday." Both of her predictions came true!

Carl was a graduate of the Combs College of Music and he had previously been a member of the Atlanta Symphony. He did audition the following year for the National Symphony and was given a position for two years, filling in for a permanent member of the orchestra who had Army duty. In 1957, he auditioned for the Cathedral Choir in which he both sang and played flute. As Lyn describes it, "Carl began 'hanging around' the cathedral between flute pupils, his free-lance orchestra commitments, and his American University classes. . ." Helping a woodworking craftsman from England, he attracted the attention of Dean Sayre, himself a craftsman with wood. The Dean believed Carl should have a cathedral shop in which to work.

It would be easier to list the things that Carl found he could not do rather than the things he did. His media were wood, wrought iron, stone, painting, polychroming, mechanics, designing, music, invention—the list can go on. It would be improper to call him a "Jack of all trades"; that implies somone who tinkers. A better description would be, "The cathedral's prodigy in residence." There is even a carved grotesque of him, complete with flute, in the cathedral fabric.

Both Lyn and Carl are natives of Philadelphia. Carl was the son of Lyn's piano teacher and they both sang in the Mendelssohn Club. Christened Evelyn Goodwin, Lyn worked at the University of Pennsylvania, Georgia Tech, and the University of Alabama before coming to Washington. At the cathedral, she served as secretary to Dean Sayre, later became Executive Secretary for the National Cathedral Association, and still later did product development for the Cathedral Museum Shop. She also served for a period as Director of Volunteers for Maryland's Public Broadcasting Network. Because she had been intimately involved with the installation of two previous Presiding Bishops, she was recalled to help coordinate the installation of Presiding Bishop John Allin.

Retiring from the cathedral in 1986, the Tuckers now reside in Pine Beach, New Jersey. Lyn continues her service to the cathedral as Chair, South New Jersey Region, National Cathedral Association. She travels to area churches making new friends for the association. Carl has not changed. He still teaches flute to his students and is associated with several community music groups. In a continuation of his cathedral experiences, he designed and built an addition to their home.

The following stories attest to their active and interesting careers with the cathedral.

The Dean's Secretary

Lyn will tell you that the telephone can be a most frustrating instrument!

When the Tuckers came to Washington, Lyn found a job at George Washington University. This was enjoyable, but she really wanted to work at the cathedral. She applied for a position, but there were no openings.

It was about two years later that she applied again at the cathedral. This time she was called in for an interview in one of the schools. She was offered a position and she asked to think about it and then call back. She really wanted to work in the cathedral's worship department, not in one of the schools. However, it came closer to what she wanted to do than the position at the university. At least she would be on the cathedral close and if a position that she wanted became available, she would be in a place most likely to take advantage of it. She called the school to accept the position. The line was busy. Telephones can be so frustrating!

While waiting, she telephoned the cathedral Business Manager one more time. "I'm glad you called, Mrs. Tucker," said John Bayless. "I just learned that the Dean's secretary is leaving. Could you come in and see us?"

Then on the other hand, the telephone can be a most helpful and rewarding piece of equipment. Lyn got her position!

The Cover for the Font

Bethlehem Chapel had been dedicated to the memory of Bishop Satterlee, the first bishop of the Washington Diocese. It seemed altogether appropriate, therefore that Resurrection Chapel should be dedicated to the memory of the second bishop of the Washington Diocese, Bishop Harding. At the Harding dedication, alas, there had been no baptismal font. The first font that had been delivered was unacceptable. The Building Committee rejected it, and it became a bird bath at the deanery.

The second font was much better; it had been executed well by the artist. There was much ornamentation on the sides of the limestone font including a rope that circled its base, as if it would bind the vessel together. Now that the new font was in place, it should be dedicated too. When the Harding family was invited to attend, they observed that no cover had been provided for the font. A cover must be obtained, but there were no longer any funds available since the chapel budget had been spent.

Cover of the Baptismal Font in Resurrection Chapel, carved by Carl Tucker.

This was before Carl Tucker had been provided with a work shop at the cathedral; his many talents still were dormant. He was asked to consider making a cover for the font and he agreed. Lyn recalls his coming home to their efficiency apartment on Pennsylvania Avenue and spreading out the oak boards and wood carving tools on their rug. He had not had great experience with wood carving and he learned a great deal about carving with the grain of the wood as opposed to carving cross grain. But he did complete the cover, even fabricated a rope to surround the lid that matched the stone rope surrounding the font. When he had finished the carving, he sank a heavy circular piece of metal in the center of the cover to which he affixed a large metal ring to serve as a handle that folds down to lie on the circular metal center. If the ring is raised and allowed to drop against the metal top, it results in a resounding tone that fills the chapel much as the peal of a bell.

Dean Sayre dedicated the font and its cover. As he intoned each person of the Trinity at the benediction he raised the metal handle and allowed it to drop as if it were a Sanctus pealing its emphasis to his words.

The Myth of Michelangelo

Michelangelo did not paint the ceiling of the Sistene Chapel while lying on his back. Of that Carl Tucker is certain. He knows from experience that one does not paint on one's back.

He had been asked to paint the ceilings under the balconies at the entrances to the cathedral from the north and south transepts. Since he had heard the stories concerning Michelangelo's ordeal he was prepared to suffer accordingly. What he discovered was that lying on one's back on the scaffold is neither comfortable nor efficient. Lying on his back, he could not see his paint pots. He had no way of knowing how far he was dipping his brush into the paint nor what color of paint he was using. He got as much paint on himself as he did on the ceiling. He did not have control of the situation.

Obtaining an old chair, he sawed ten inches from the back legs and eight inches from the front. This gave him support on an inclined plane. He also constructed a small tray in front of the chair where he could place all of his paint pots. Being able to see the pots, he could see clearly which one he was using as well as the quantity of paint on his brush. It also gave him a better base for painting and his hand was steadier. By being better able to see further from the elevated plane, it also gave him a better perspective of the total project.

The work at the south transept entrance was completed by Carl in 1974 from a design for the ceiling that had been prepared by the artist Kurt Landberg. In 1985, Carl was commissioned to design and paint the ceiling under the north balcony. It was the final task he performed for the cathedral prior to his retirement.

Mr. Frohman had insisted that Carl use no template for painting all of the decorations in the many different shades and colors. He wanted the painting to be freehand. There is nothing about the painting that looks to be machine-processed. It is obviously work by an artist and it is worth bending one's neck to observe. And if you go to the south balcony, stand with your back against the west wrought-iron gate, and look up at the second beam, you will see the artist's signature and the date.

But there is no way that Michelangelo painted the ceiling of the Sistene Chapel lying on his back. Carl Tucker will tell you, the story is pure myth!

*Carl Tucker hand-painting
the ceiling at the north transept portal.*

Photo by Patrick J. Plunkett

Frustrating the CIA

Lyn was working with the National Cathedral Association on Mt. St. Alban, when her recently widowed father came for a visit. He was not to be enticed to remain at home each day while both Lyn and Carl were at the cathedral so he came to Lyn's office to help with whatever volunteer tasks presented themselves.

During a lull in the activity, he wandered out to other areas of the close and he visited the Chapel of the Good Shepherd, the one part of the cathedral that was kept open for private prayers and meditation 24 hours each day. He saw a note on the altar that had been left there for some nameless person, a brief little note of apology, but he thought it certainly was written in a most pedestrian manner and he felt it should be embellished.

Taking the note with him back to Lyn's office, he obtained some of her colored pencils. Being an outstanding calligrapher, he reproduced the note with his better calligraphy and illuminated it with the colors. It was a superb example of penmanship when he returned it to the altar in the chapel.

Some time later, Lyn was reading a novel in which CIA operatives left messages in code in the Good Shepherd Chapel for their contacts. She was momentarily aghast! Had the efforts of a mighty agency in the federal government been frustrated by her father? Was it possible that the wrong message could have been sent to some important ally? It was frightening to realize that all of this could have happened through a very innocent intent on the part of her father, to improve on the penmanship of a note writer.

The Cathedral Staff Family

In small organizations where there is strong leadership and a feeling of achievement toward a commonly recognized goal, organization morale tends to soar. In such instances staff members seem to react much as members of a closely knit family. Lyn describes many such instances in the late 1950s and the early 1960s that affected the cathedral staff.

✚ Richard Feller had a very delightful young secretary who was to travel to England to be married. There was a shower for her at one of the homes and the entire staff at the cathedral attended. When she went to the airport to depart, again all of the staff went with her to see her off. They were her family.

✚ Some members of the staff humorously took the first lines of certain hymns and applied them to persons of the staff. Lyn remembered several.

. . . One of the secretaries drove a very large beige colored Cadillac. For her, "Ride on, ride on in majesty."

. . . For the Verger, "He leadeth me."

. . . For the chief electrician, "Some times a light surprises."

. . . The principal hostess at the College of Preachers who provided repasts *par excellence*, "My God, and is Thy table spread!"

✦ When Lyn and Carl purchased a home and decided to quit the life of "cliff dwellers," one of their staff friends picked them up to take them to a movie. Instead, they went to the deanery where all of the staff was assembled to shower them with gifts for their new home.

✦ Choirmaster Wayne Dirksen stood at the foot of the parclose stairs, inspecting the choir boys going upstairs for the Sunday morning service. One of the youngsters, Rick Dirksen, was sent back by his father because he was wearing white socks, not the black socks prescribed. Young Rick went back to the choir room sobbing, where Carl Tucker was vesting. Seeing the trouble, he exchanged socks with young Rick.

After the service, Carl admitted to Wayne Dirksen what had happened. Dirksen's comment was, "I wondered who had been conned into a switch."

✦ On the occasion of Lyn's mother's death, the cathedral staff expressed their sympathy by giving a light fixture for the Chapel of the Good Shepherd. The fixture was fabricated by Carl, so that it became doubly meaningful.

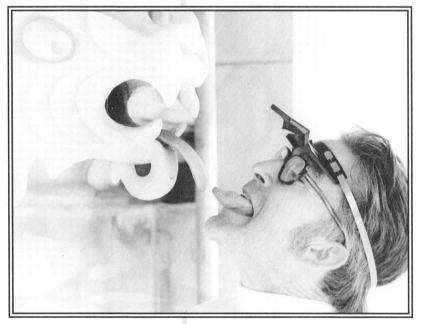

Carl Tucker inspecting a grotesque at the cathedral. Tucker is on the right.
Photo by Byron Chambers

To Build a Harpsichord

This was a fascinating experience for the students at St. Albans. They would come to the shop where Carl Tucker, the musician, became Carl Tucker, the cabinet maker and instrument designer. He was building a harpsichord. The students were not at all certain that this endeavor would succeed; they called it a "perhapsichord." Even Mr. Frohman was less than convinced that what was being undertaken would be crowned with success. "Don't worry," he reassured the enterprising harpsichordist. "If you can't play it, you can always make a desk out of it." There is nothing like having a supportive audience!

Carl had heard Paul Callaway playing a harpsichord. After a close inspection, he decided that he could make one too. Working in his spare time in his shop on the cathedral grounds, he fashioned an instrument using plywood, shoe leather and plastic keys. He used razor blades to shave the small pieces of shoe leather into the leather plectra that pluck the strings. It was painstaking work but when it was finished it worked beautifully. It was transported to the pit in Lisner Auditorium where Paul Callaway played it in concert, and the program announced that the instrument had been created and provided by Mr. Carl Tucker. Mozart never sounded better to at least two members of the audience.

Carl spent $147.65 and more than 600 hours of his time to complete the instrument. He has not accepted any orders for additional harpsichords; "perhaps" he had nothing more to prove.

The Nativity

Richard Wayne Dirksen was always composing. He has probably written as much contemporary church music as any living composer. It was not unusual, therefore, when he called Carl Tucker and asked him to come to the choir with his flute. Dirksen had a new composition, "The Nativity," a selection for choir and flute. He planned for it to be presented at the Christmas season and he wanted Carl to play the flute solo.

It was so successful that it has been repeated many times since and the music has now been published. Oh yes, Dirksen wanted to dedicate the composition to Lyn.

It has been so recorded.

Lights in the Children's Chapel

No matter how carefully one plans the construction of a cathedral, something seems always to be left out—to have been overlooked. The Children's Chapel was one of those areas.

In the original plans for the chapel, no provision had been made for a baptismal font. This was a major concern, a font would have to be provided. And it is fortunate that this was done, for baptisms are held at Children's Chapel font probably more frequently than all other fonts in the cathedral combined.

A font was installed with a temporary light above it. Carl described the light as looking like a "three-pound coffee can soldered to an inverted funnel and painted black." It was not a thing of joy or of beauty.

On each side of the altar in the chapel, a niche had been cut into the stone wall to provide a socket in which a bulb could be screwed to provide light at the altar. The shields that softened the lights had disappeared. There has been a problem from time to time, with visitors taking items as souvenirs. Again, Carl Tucker was called. Could he provide appropriate light fixtures for Children's Chapel? Yes, of course. His answer was always yes.

The great Samuel Yellin had designed and fabricated the wrought iron screen for the chapel, making everything child size and with features that would delight both children and their parents. He had also fabricated the two light fixtures just inside the gate. Using the design of the two Yellin fixtures, Carl designed and fabricated a wrought-iron chandelier to hang over the font. He contributed it as a memorial to Lyn's grandmother, Emma Goodwin.

Going back to the earlier records in the archives, he found the shop drawings used by Yellin for the two small hinged light shields for the side lights over the altar. Using the original drawings, he was able to reproduce the original Yellin fixtures and to install them.

The Head of Helen Keller

There was to be a visitation by a group of blind persons for a special service at the cathedral. How nice it would be if they could see with their fingers, the head of Helen Keller. But that beautifully carved south corbel completed by Constantine Seferlis, in the National Cathedral Association bay outer aisle was twelve to fourteen feet above the floor level. It would not be possible to provide any kind of platform that would allow people to gain access to the carving without great danger to themselves.

Carl Tucker had a solution.

He had to be certain that there would be no damage to the corbel. And that meant that whatever solution he employed it must not be anything that could be absorbed into the surface of the stone or that would discolor it. He had to perform the research very carefully in order to prepare a new head using the corbel as the basis for the face. He used a number of different materials—wire screen, plaster, silicone, rubber sheeting. There was debris all around the area in the outer aisle. He remembers seeing Richard Feller walking by, looking, shaking his head and walking on, saying nothing. In the end he was able to duplicate the corbel.

When the assembly visited the cathedral, Helen Keller was there awaiting them. The head is still on display and it is one of those items that visitors are invited to touch.

Copy of the Helen Keller Corbel.
This remains on display with invitations
to the public to touch.

To Design 'Scotch' Gothic

Philip Frohman was asked to design a completion of the cathedral's Administration Building. At the time, there was only a two-story elevation of concrete blocks painted white. Another full story was desired, and the total building was to be encased in limestone.

This was to be a building that adjoined the cathedral. Since the cathedral was Gothic in style, we should have an administration building worthy of its association with the original model. Frohman planned to design a building that was true Gothic. There were to be pointed arches, the customary crenelations and reveals, gargoyles and pinnacles.

But this was not what the authorities had in mind. Faced with the likelihood of acquiring a debt for the rest of the construction on Mt. St. Alban, it was considered that restraint in the decor of the Administration Building would be a virtue, highly to be desired. Accordingly, Mr. Frohman was asked to design a more modest facility, devoid of pretensions to grandeur.

This second attempt was very well received, and the building was constructed in accordance with his design. When asked to assign an architectural style to the building, Frohman winced and scornfully proclaimed it to be "Scotch Gothic!"

An Appeal by a Byrdwatcher

Lyn Tucker had heard music by William Byrd at the cathedral for four Sundays in succession. She was less than enthusiastic about his music and when saturated by it as she had been, she sent the following doggerel to Paul Callaway, the cathedral's organist and choirmaster. Of course, Lyn was not above being something of a punster herself, as one will note from the title of her work:

TO A-MUSE

Hail to thee, blithe spirit!
(Byrd thou never wert.)
Tho' here you'll always hear it-
From Callaway - in skirt.

Byrdbrained all our 'masters;
They go for Lassus, too.
Purcellian trumpet blasters
Play their loud tattoo.

O, for good old Stanford-
Even in B-flat-
Or how about Brother James' Air?
What's so wrong with that?

Plainsong tunes surround us,
And Sowerby's so sour!
Who's to save "the people"
At Cathedral's Evensong hour?

Mercy, Dr. Calla-
Way up there in space!
Mercy, Wayne and Norman!
Adopt a gayer pace!

Precentor, hear our pleading!
O, let our cry come nigh!
The price of all this purity,
We think, comes awfully high

Installing a Bredlow Gate

Tom Bredlow, of Tucson, Arizona, was one of a long line of superb wrought-iron artists who have obtained commissions at the cathedral. His first commission had been to duplicate a candle holder at the high altar, a piece by the great Samuel Yellin. When he completed this successfully, he was given other commissions.

Several of his commissions were for wrought-iron gates. When the first gate arrived at the cathedral, it was accompanied by two long strips of brown wrapping paper, on which the artist had written detailed instructions on how the gate should be installed. Carl read the instructions and then proceeded to install the gate as he thought it should be done.

He laid out the gate and the side pieces, fully assembled, with the gate three thirty-seconds of an inch higher than the side pieces. This disparity was to allow for the gate to settle when its weight was fully felt by gravity's pull after it had been installed. He drilled the holes in the wall, built up small "bird's-nests" of plaster around the holes, and then filled the holes with Rockite, a registered fast setting concrete substance. When the Rockite had set, he chiseled away the plaster so that there is virtually nothing visible at the holes other than the surrounding limestone.

Bredlow was delighted when he saw the installed gate even though he never knew that Carl had disregarded his instructions. He sent a box of wrought-iron roses to Jack Fanfani with instructions that he distribute them to several persons at the cathedral. Carl received one.

Odds 'n Ends

✢ "Mrs. Sayre was very pregnant with their fourth child and the students in the schools wondered whether the child was to be a girl or a boy. They even started rumors, that if male, St. Albans would have a day of holiday; if female, the National Cathedral School for Girls would be so blessed. The girls were convinced that they were to be the recipients of this boon and each week at chapel, they sang the hymn, "Come labor on." Alas, it was a boy.

✢ It was in the winter. The weather was cold but the construction crews had to finish pouring the concrete floor in the central tower for the carillon. The bells were coming and the floor must be completed to receive and hold them. The crews had been working since seven in the morning and it was now nearly 11 in the evening. Lyn remembers Carl going to the "Little Tavern" up Wisconsin Avenue, buying all of the hamburgers and coffee available and then climbing up the scaffold to give it to the workmen.

✚ Lyn recalls the visit by the Archbishop of Canterbury (he was number 100). She was entrusted to guard the Archbishop's jewel encrusted crosier. She was amused that it was carried in a small metal valise, still labeled "Archbishop of York." That had been his previous position.

✚ Mr. Frohman represented the precise manifestation of a Victorian gentleman. No one ever called him anything other than Mr. Frohman. In the same sense, he never addressed any other workman at the cathedral without the Mr. His manner conveyed a sense of dignity and respect that he felt for others and that he invited in return.

✚ When the very lovely Garth fountain was installed, it was not possible for Dean Sayre to look out of his office window on the second floor of the cloister without seeing the name of the artist, George Tsutakawa, prominently displayed on one of the petals. It had been designed so that it would not be too visible from the ground level, but from above it stood out almost as clearly as if it had been an advertising slogan. Carl was called. He removed the offending letters and then reinstalled the artist's name on a less visible part of the fountain.

✚ Mr. Frohman always wore his silver-colored tin hat. Everyone else had substituted the new plastic hard hats, to guard against the stray hot wire that might give one a nasty shock. Although he was 82 years old, Mr. Frohman continued to climb the scaffold, going up on the building every day to check the construction's progress. And he continued to wear his silver hat until the day he died.

✚ Carl believes it was a mistake to have put electrical outlets in the marble floor of the cathedral. Janitors and others remove the cover plates to plug in equipment and then forget to replace the plates so that wax, grout and dirt get into the openings and cake up the plugs. There are several areas where electricity is not available because the boxes have been misused.

✚ Carl recalls Paul Callaway practicing early in the morning for a special organ concert he was to give in Philadelphia with the Philadelphia Philharmonic. The score was an original composition by Samuel Barber and the pages were large and cumbersome. Carl would come in each morning and turn pages for Callaway until he finally had memorized the score.

✦ Piccolo came to live with the Tuckers. Carl was working on a scaffold in front of the cathedral on a cold day in December when he saw a small dog shivering on the ground. He tried to find an owner but no one claimed the little black dog with white spots. Of indeterminate and unspecific origin, the dog resembled nothing so much as Carl's ebony piccolo with its eight white buttons. No, we were not going to suggest that the dog played the piccolo. The little "cathedralpup" adopted the Tuckers, however, and agreed to remain. Curiously, she responded whenever she heard the cathedral bells, and this continued for the rest of her life.

Working in a Gothic Building

There are seldom ever routine work experiences associated with a Gothic building. It is best always to expect the unexpected. It is what you are likely to experience.

The doors at the north transept had been little better than rough shed doors, just something to keep out prowlers, animals and the cold until the solid wood doors being manufactured in England arrived and were installed. They did arrive, in the middle of January and the weather was COLD! Carl was called to install them.

There were two solid bronze frames manufactured locally that were to be installed, one for each of the two doors. It became obvious immediately that when the measurements had been taken, the person had measured the west door only, not the east door. The two frames were identical in size; the door openings were not.

The west door frame was installed without difficulty. Everything went in very easily. The west door was hung and Carl then addressed the east door. Nothing fit. The east door opening was about one-and-one-half inches narrower and it would need to be enlarged. Fortunately, there were enough stone carvers around with their equipment so that before too much time had expired, they enlarged the opening and Carl was able to fit in the bronze frame for the east door.

It still did not fit. Carl had to fabricate a wedge of bronze and hammer it in place with a sledge hammer to create a tight fit. Finally, the door was hung and everything worked just right; except that there was no opening in the door frame for the lock keeper. The door could not be locked. Carl had to drill an opening in the frame for the lock keeper in order to close and lock the door.

Finally, at two in the morning, Carl was able to go home reflecting as he did so, how the great beauty of Gothic construction seems always to be accompanied by so many trials and tribulations.

Piccolo and friend.

Treating the Majestus

*Canopy for the Majestus
designed and fabricated by Carl Tucker
under the watchful eye
of Architect Philip Frohman.*

Photo by H. Byron Chambers

Roger Morigi had completed carving the Majestus, and it could be viewed in its place in the reredos. There was a striking difference in color between the Caen stone from France, used for the original reredos, and the new limestone from Texas used for the Majestus. The Texas stone was noticeably lighter, so much so that it was objectionable to many observers. Something had to be done to darken the Majestus.

There were conferences to determine how best to accomplish the change. It has been told for years around the cathedral that Carl used a weak solution of tea to darken the stone. Carl disclaims that story. It was discussed as a possibility but he had rejected it. Once tea is applied to the stone it has been permanently altered. He did not want any responsibility for an action that would permanently alter Walker Hancock's sculpture. Tea was not used.

Carl went to several art supply stores and obtained artist colors in powder form and blended them until he had a mixture that he believed would properly match the reredos. He then proceded to dust the Majestus with his mixture that served to darken it just enough so that the difference in color was barely recognizable.

Subsequently, he was asked to clean the reredos. This he did with a small hand held vacuum and an assortment of brushes, but he was careful not to change the condition of the Majestus.

The Canopy for the Majestus

Unfortunately, the canopy to cover the Majestus had been carved and installed many years earlier. It was a mistake to have done so. But no one could have known in those early days that it would take so many years to find a sculptor who could provide an acceptable statue. Now, when the Majestus was finally completed, the canopy was completely out of scale. It had to be changed.

There were several meetings to discuss the matter. Everyone agreed that change was required but no one knew what had to be done. At one meeting, Carl Tucker suggested the changes he thought would be required to move and modify the canopy. The next day Howard Trevillian, who was an assistant architect to Mr. Frohman, came to see Carl and to tell him that they had decided to accept his suggestions. But there was a dilemma. It would require about 20 architectural drawings that would consume an inordinate amount of time. Could Carl build a model without the drawings? Yes, of course.

Carl worked in his shop. He had the reference points he needed and he began to put the model together. Each day, Mr. Frohman would come into his shop to see what progress he had made. Carl was concerned, for the several steps into his shop were not the most solid. He took several reject limestone blocks and built steps, erected a handrail and provided a better approach for the elderly architect. Each day Mr. Frohman would come. He would suggest that one rib be tighter, another moved to open the vaulting. But he followed the construction of the model carefully until it was completed.

Finally the model was taken to the chancel to the place it was to occupy in the reredos. Everyone was pleased with it, The fit was perfect. The stone carvers executed the canopy, and the model was returned to Carl.

Typical of the man, Mr. Frohman made one more trip to the Tucker shop. "Mr. Tucker," he said. "For 40 years I have worried about that canopy and how we would be able to make it fit. And now you have solved it." Carl admits, his feet didn't touch the ground the rest of the day!

Pipes that do not Radiate nor Heat

The radiant heating generally worked very well in the cathedral where the workmen installed it correctly. In the west end, however, there is one area where there is no heat and where there never will be any.

When the concrete underlayment of the nave floor had been poured back in the 1920s, it had been done improperly. It has never been established why, but as the floor progressed from the east to the west it rose perceptibly so that not only was the floor not level, it was not even at the same elevation. There was no alternative; jack hammers were brought in and with great noise and even greater distress, portions of the floor were removed in the west end.

This was the first problem.

In the earlier construction and the first application of the radiant heating concept, pipe under the marble floor was all wrought-iron pipe. It had been made in England at the only manufactory in the world where one could obtain such pipe, and it had worked well. But with the advent of many different kinds of plastic pipe, the company in England had abandoned the manufacture of wrought-iron pipe and no one else had sought to replace them. It was not possible to obtain it.

This was the second problem.

Consulting engineers did a very detailed search of the kinds of pipe available and that they believed would work well. They selected a pipe of a bronze alloy that was believed to be exceptionally long lasting and that would work well to provide the radiant heating to the west end floor. Because the floor had been poured too high in the west end, crews used the jack hammers to cut trenches in the concrete to lay the new pipe and connect it to the heating system.

That was the third problem.

After the marble floor was laid in place, and Clerk of the Works Feller was satisfied that the problems had been resolved there suddenly came a flood of water into the museum storage area below the west end. An investigation by the consulting engineers established the reason for it: a bacteria had attacked the pipe from the inside and had eaten through the pipe. Feller has never had what he considers to be a completely satisfactory explanation of how bacteria attack metal and destroy it.

Nevertheless, say the engineers, that was the fourth problem.

To take up the marble floor and correct the problems would cost millions of dollars and would cause the cathedral to be closed for a lengthy period of time. Both conditions would be prohibitive. Since people do not sit in the areas that have no radiant heating, and the heating from the other areas appears to be adequate for the building, the heated water was cut off from the west end and the radiant heating abandoned.

That was the solution.

Lock pin fabricated for a wrought-iron gate in the south transept.

Controlling the Lock Pin

The wrought-iron gate just to the east of the south transept entrance had a lock that was different from almost all of the other gates in the cathedral. But when the cathedral commissions an artist to fabricate a gate, he also determines the kind of lock that the gate should have and fabricates it as well. This gate had a lock pin that slipped into a hole in the wall and when it was in place, the lock could be activated with a key to secure it. The trouble was that people were not accustomed to moving a lock pin back and forth. They left it open and when the gate was closed, the pin began defacing the stone wall. This was not acceptable. Call for Carl Tucker.

He designed a very attractive wrought iron trough, carved out an area in the stone where it could be inserted and it was installed. Now if one leaves the pin extended, it is automatically retracted when the gate is closed. It is the kind of solution that any of us would have chosen, if only we had thought of it and had the ability to carry it off.

Working in a Cathedral

Carl says it is difficult to describe the sense of fulfillment and enjoyment that he experienced in working at the cathedral. He mentions the satisfaction from his encounters with Mr. Frohman, Mr. Feller, Mr. Bayless, Mr. Fanfani, Mr. Trevillian, Dr. Callaway, Dean Sayre—all outstanding persons who made working at the cathedral a real privilege. He had the opportunity to find places where something should be supplied or fabricated that he was able to do. Frequently he was asked to undertake certain tasks; in other instances he could function independently.

Dean Sayre came to his shop one day and said, "Carl, you have the best job at the cathedral." Carl saw no reason to disagree.

Miscellaneous

I t is to be expected that in an undertaking such as this, the odd story will surface that should be included, even though its attribution is questionable. It is possible to ascertain its veracity yet no one will claim it. The only place where such stories may be incorporated is in a miscellaneous section. To a large degree, they are orphans; therefore I shall adopt them.

In several of these stories, I was a participant. In some, it was information that I stumbled across in doing the research associated with this volume. In others, well, it's a miscellaneous section.

The Herb Cottage,
built originally to be a Baptistry
for the Cathedral.

Photo by Beverly Rezneck

The Herb Cottage

In the early decades of the Washington Cathedral's construction, it had been planned to provide a total immersion font for baptisms. For many reasons, the concept of a total immersion font was not acceptable to the cathedral clergy and the idea was abandoned, but not before a separate structure had been erected at the southwest corner of the cathedral to serve this purpose. When the idea was abandoned, it became necessary to designate an alternate use for the building. This was done by a most remarkable woman, Mrs. Florence Brown Bratenahl, who in her own right contributed much to the history of the Washington Cathedral.

As was stated earlier, the first dean of the cathedral was The Very Reverend George C. F. Bratenahl. His wife, who had studied landscape architecture and design, had also been associated with the eminent landscape architect Frederick Law Olmsted, Jr. who had been employed to do the initial design for the cathedral close. When his contract expired, Mrs. Bratenahl replaced him. Not only did she lay out the plan for the Bishop's Garden, she also developed the design for the Pilgrim Steps that lead from the Washington equestrian statue to the south transept.

Another of Mrs. Bratenahl's interests was in growing herbs. She was able to persuade a friend and associate who owned a farm in Maryland to produce quantities of fresh herbs. When the Baptistery was no longer required for baptisms, Mrs. Bratenahl used the building for the sale of these herbs by All Hallows Guild. She brought quantities of both fresh and dried herbs from the farm and gave the proceeds from their sales to the construction of the cathedral. Over time, the building became known as "The Herb Cottage." The facility continues to be managed by All Hallows Guild and now also offers a variety of other items for sale.

The St. Paul Sculpture

Probably no issue brought before the Building Committee in 1982 was more controversial than the proposed statue for St. Paul. The statue, to be placed at the main portal for the southwest tower, had been commissioned to Frederick Hart and he had submitted his proposed model to the Building Committee for approval.

Hart had selected the story in the Book of Acts as the basis for his model. In this story, Paul had lost his sight temporarily on the way to Damascus and was sightless for several days until his vision was restored. The proposed sculpture showed Paul walking, one hand extended to his front and his eyes closed. The closed eyes concerned several members of the committee; they wanted the eyes open. The members discussed this issue for the better part of two hours. Finally, Chairman Richard Feller called on one member who had been quiet during the discussion. What was his thought concerning the eyes?

"The eyes are no more important than the hands or feet," the member replied. "Rather than look at parts of the sculpture, we should consider the work as a whole. What emotion or feeling does the statue convey? In my judgment, any statue of St. Paul needs to show two things. First, as the Church's first missionary, Paul was always moving. He visited many places and, therefore, the statue should show or imply motion. It does. Secondly, Paul was the Church's first intellectual. The statue should convey a sense of a thinking being. Again, it does. I am satisfied with the artist's concept."

Perhaps the members of the committee were weary but they approved the artist's model. And so today, St. Paul faces those approaching the cathedral with his eyes closed. Somehow, it seems to say to the visitor, "You must see for Him. Look only for those things that are worthy of His vision!"

The St. Paul Statue at the southwest portal. Sculptor, Frederick Hart; Carver, Vincent Palumbo.
Photo by Carol M. Highsmith

Angelo Lualdi

In August 1988, the great-grandson of Sculptor Angelo Lualdi came to see his ancestor's creation. During the 1930s, one of the principal areas of creative activity in the cathedral was that of sculpting and then carving the reredos at the High Altar. Sculptor Angelo Lualdi, living at that time in Cambridge, Massachusetts, had been awarded a commission to prepare plaster models for many of the statues to be placed in the niches of the reredos.

It is generally conceded that people tend to be most creative in the environment that is most compatible with their artistic temperament. Signor Lualdi considered the commission for the cathedral to be a very important undertaking and he believed that in order to do the job properly, he needed to return to Italy. Fortunately, the cathedral administrators have been supportive of this point of view. Not only did he return to his native Florence and set up a studio where he prepared the plaster models for the many statues in the reredos, but he established a precedent of sorts. In later years, Senor Enrique Monjo who was given a commission for the angel models at the south transept, returned to his native Barcelona, Spain and completed the models in his Spanish studios. Still later, Herr Ulrich Henn designed the massive west portal bronze gates at his studio in Germany.

Artists and workmen at the cathedral have come from many nations and nationalities, but a quantity of work has been completed in other countries as well. This is a most appropriate approach for a cathedral that has as its motto, "A House of Prayer for all People."

The bronze Lincoln statue in the Lincoln Bay of the nave. Sculptor was Walter Hancock.

Hancock, on the Lincoln Statue

The sculptor of the Lincoln Statue in the northwest corner of the nave, Walker Hancock, was a man deeply interested in the play of lights on his works. He had come to Washington Cathedral to see how the Lincoln statue appeared in the spotlights that had been placed on the piers and directed toward the statue. There was a modest amount of moving the sculpture and redirecting the lights until everyone concerned with the exercise was satisfied.

As the participants in the lighting activity began to drift away, Mr. Hancock turned to a bystander and asked, "When you look at the Lincoln statue, what do you think of, how does it appeal to you?"

"It's the hands," the person responded. "I find the hands to be compelling. In one sense, Lincoln was a very introspective person, a person who valued his privacy and retained a significant amount of his innermost thoughts that he shared with no one. The position of the left hand seems to say, 'This is the private Lincoln; this part of the person is not for viewing'.

"But in another sense, Lincoln was a very compassionate and caring person; he reached out to people, he wanted to be a part of other people's concerns. The right hand manifests this part of Lincoln's person in that it is reaching out."

"That is precisely what I wanted to express," said Hancock.

This was flattering to the bystander, that he had been able to read the mind of a very famous artist in creating his sculpture. Later he came to understand that Mr. Hancock obtained other people's opinions better to appreciate what the public saw in his work but also he wanted to make them feel good about expressing themselves. Hancock would probably have been enthusiastic about almost anything that may have been said by the bystander.

Training Bell Ringers

It was in October 1963 that the peal bells were installed in the central tower of the cathedral. The installation was accomplished by Harry Parkes from the Whitechapel Foundry in England. Not until they were installed, however, did it become apparent that no one in Washington knew how to ring such bells. In fact, there were only two places in the United States where peal bells were being rung: at the Kent and Groton preparatory schools in New England. Change ringing was an English tradition. It was entirely foreign to the Washington area. After Parkes completed the installation of the bells in the tower, he extended his stay for another two weeks in order to train a group of about 15, consisting of adults at the cathedral and students at St. Albans School, in the proper method of pulling the ropes and ringing the bells. A book was provided that explained the intricacies of change ringing but the group had very little understanding of how this was accomplished. More instruction was essential. In May 1964, a group of ten bell ringers from England came to Washington as guests of Washington Cathedral, to ring the bells for the dedication of the central tower and to give instruction to the local ringers. These English ringers had been selected by John Chilcott, captain of the ringers at St. Paul's Cathedral in London, because they were outstanding teachers or well known and skilled bell ringers. All but Harry Parkes were members of the Ancient Society of College Youths, a famous bell ringing society in the British Isles. This group remained in Washington for a week and gave excellent instruction to the local group. While they were here, they gave a demonstration for the students of the National Cathedral School. That inspired Headmistress Katherine Lee to establish a group of young women bell ringers known as the Whitechapel Guild. This group continues today under the direction of Richard S. Dirksen.

During October 1964, arrangements were completed for a very experienced bell ringer, a man named Fred Price, to come to Washington from England and remain in residence for six months, to give additional instruction to the original group of ringers and to train many new ringers. After his departure, Dean Sayre appointed Richard S. Dirksen as Ringing Master at Washington National Cathedral and charged him to establish and direct programs to train bell ringers and to provide for competence in change ringing. Rick remained in this position until his retirement in September 1993.

Change ringing is entirely an English tradition that originated in the 17th century and is practiced in most of the major English cathedrals and many of the Anglican churches. Due in large measure to the influence of the cathedral's ringing program and its ringers, it is fast becoming an American tradition as well.

Laurel and Hardy in Construction

It is difficult to believe that the slapstick antics of Laurel and Hardy would manifest themselves in the serious business of building a cathedral yet that is precisely what happened. Otto Epps, for over 30 years a faithful and dependable mason's assistant, told of an incident that occurred many years ago. There was a stone mason, who shall be nameless, who was faced with the requirement to set a stone in a location that he could not reach from the scaffold that was then in place. Fortunately, the location was only a matter of about eight to ten feet above the ground and although a fall of that distance could result in injuries to the person, it would not be life-threatening.

In order for the mason to reach the stone and to work on it, he obtained a board that he placed perpendicular to the stone wall but that would reach beyond it, so that he could stand on the end of the board to set the stone. In order to secure the board, he asked his helper to stand on the other end, so that his weight would serve to counter-balance that of the mason. This in itself was an invitation to disaster; however, neither the mason nor his helper saw any potential problem in the arrangement.

The mason was in the process of setting his stone when he asked his helper to hand him his level. The helper stepped off the board to obtain the level, the board tipped up and the mason fell to the ground. Laurel and Hardy could hardly have invented a more likely episode for their antics.

The 10 English bell ringers. Harry Parks is at the far left, and he has just pulled the rope for the tenor bell.

Photo by Stewart Brothers

The Salute to Vietnam Veterans

It was during November 10-14, 1982 that a massive recognition of the Vietnam Veterans was held in the nation's capital to coincide with the official dedication of the Vietnam Veterans Memorial. The observance was crowded with events to honor and recognize the service and sacrifice of those who fought in America's longest war. A lengthy parade down Constitution Avenue preceded the official dedication ceremony and a number of lesser events took place during the evenings. The occasion had been planned by the Vietnam Veterans Memorial Fund and they also requested Washington National Cathedral to provide the location for a three-day vigil and to have a Sunday morning memorial service.

The vigil consisted of a continuous reading of the names of those who gave their lives or who remained missing in action. As was explained, a person's name is his most sacred possession, both in life and in death. It was appropriate that the reading of those names should occur in the National Cathedral. Held in War Memorial Chapel and then Bethlehem Chapel, the vigil continued day and night until all 57,939 names had been read. More than 250 volunteer readers, serving in groups of two or three for 30 minutes, read all of the names alphabetically until all names were read. The vigil required 56 hours to complete. Each quarter hour was marked by the reading of a prayer from the Episcopal, Roman Catholic, Protestant, Jewish or Unitarian traditions.

The volunteer readers came from all parts of the country. In many cases they were friends or family members of someone who did not return. They were young and old, black and white, male and female, dressed in business suits or in jeans or uniforms. More than 12,000 visitors came to participate.

In the Sunday morning Eucharist and Memorial Service, the Rev. Theodore H. Evans, himself a Vietnam Veteran, who had been priest-in-charge of the Mekong Missionary District, was the preacher. Also participating were John Wheeler, Jan Scruggs, and Robert Doubek, the three who established the Vietnam Veterans Memorial Fund, and who also organized the Salute to Vietnam Veterans.

Provost Charles Perry said that he had known few times in the history of the cathedral so fraught with emotion and human concern. It was altogether appropriate that the cathedral should play a leading role in helping to heal the wounds and to reconcile the estrangement for many resulting from the Vietnam War.

The Helen Keller Plaque

Of all the famous persons who have been interred in the cathedral, Helen Keller is one of the best known and most highly respected. Few persons have had the physical handicaps with which she was born, and certainly none has overcome them to achieve as much.

In 1980 a bronze plaque was installed on one of the large piers in the St. Joseph of Arimathea Chapel announcing that the remains of Helen Keller and her constant companion, Anne Sullivan Macy, were interred in the columbarium. Richard Feller asked a volunteer assistant in his office to initiate the arrangements for the plaque to be prepared and to be installed. In discussing the plaque, the suggestion was made that it might be cast both in English and in Braille. After all, it would certainly be appropriate to have a plaque concerning Helen Keller provided in Braille for sightless people.

On one occasion, the volunteer observed a blind woman reading the plaque and especially he noted the look of absolute ecstasy on her face at the time. If there had ever been any doubt about inscribing the announcement in both English and Braille, it would have been erased on that occasion.

In 1993, the plaque had to be replaced. The Braille had been rubbed smooth by the many people, both sighted and sightless, who had been drawn to it over the years.

Persons Interred in
Washington National Cathedral

Tradition in cathedrals throughout Europe has provided final resting places for many of those best known in the nation or the community, and especially those who have held positions of great responsibility or of special significance. In touring any cathedral in Europe one is aware of the many sarcophagi and tablet memorials of vaults that contain the dead of the centuries. To be interred in a cathedral was considered a great honor and it was sought avidly by both the great and the near-great. In many places, royalty have also been interred with very elaborate sarcophagi or statuary. It was not unusual for a monarch to commission artists to prepare a sarcophagus for him well before his death.

Probably, those most often interred in cathedrals are bishops, deans of the cathedral or clergy who held special places in the hearts of the community. If any had been canonized, then the remains most certainly have been memorialized. These memorials are impressive; they have been added for six to eight centuries so there has been adequate opportunity for them to accumulate.

By mid-1994, 174 persons had been interred in Washington Cathedral, either in the vaults under Bethlehem Chapel or St. Joseph of Arimathea Chapel, in several sarcophagi or in the columbaria. This is, indeed, a very large number considering that the cathedral is not yet one century old. Unlike other nations, America is not likely to have a large number of persons from public life interred at Washington Cathedral. Almost all statesmen of note in America begin their public careers serving their native states. Their orientations are to their states, not to the nation, and they tend to seek burial in that part of the country where they began their public lives.

It is not to be compared with Westminster Abbey, nevertheless Washington National Cathedral has some very well known and respected persons interred within its walls.

GEORGE CARL FITCH BRATENAHL. Born in Cleveland, Ohio on May 4, 1862, he grew up in Ohio and New York. He graduated from Williams College in accounting, and took employment in England. Deciding to enter the ministry, he studied in New York and was ordained on June 5, 1898. He served as Rector of St. Albans Church and greatly expanded the activities of the parish. In 1912 he was appointed Canon Precentor at the cathedral and in 1915 was elected the first dean. He was responsible for all of the early direction of the cathedral's construction and developed the initial plans for the iconography. He served as dean until his retirement in 1936. He died on February 28, 1939.

FLORENCE BROWN BRATENAHL. The wife of Dean Bratenahl, she was as distinguished as her husband in the many contributions she made to Mt. St. Alban. She had been widowed at about the same time the Dean became a widower. They were married in 1915 and Florence Bratenahl proceeded to have the house built that now bears the Bratenahl name. A very diligent student of gardening and landscape design, she took over the responsibility of the Bishop's Garden and much of the early landscape work on the close. She started the All Hallows Guild and initiated the sale of herbs at The Herb Cottage, with proceeds to go to the building fund for the cathedral. She died on May 14, 1940.

GEORGE DEWEY. Born in 1837 in Montpelier, Vermont, he graduated from the U.S. Naval Academy in Annapolis, in 1861. He served continuously in the Navy until 1899. As Admiral of the Asiatic Fleet, he destroyed the Spanish Fleet at Manila in 1898 and was instrumental in securing victory over the Spanish in the Philippines. A member of the first Building Committee at the cathedral, he was the one who made the motion accepting the plans for a Gothic cathedral as designed by Dr. George Bodley.

CORDELL HULL. He was born in Pickett County, Tennessee in 1871. He attended Cumberland University Law School and was admitted to the bar at age 19. He served in the Tennessee legislature from 1893-1897. After service in the Spanish-American War, he was a Circuit Court Judge. Elected to Congress from Tennessee in 1907, he served for 22 years with a very distinguished record. Elected to the Senate in 1931, he was appointed Secretary of State in 1933 and held this position until he resigned because of poor health in 1944. Called the "Father of the United Nations," he received the Nobel Peace Prize in 1945. He spent his declining years writing and died in 1955.

PHILIP HUBERT FROHMAN. The grandson of a well known architect who pioneered in building sky-scraper apartment buildings in New York, Philip Frohman was a child prodigy. Born in Cincinnati, Ohio in November 1887, he knew from his early youth that he would be an architect, and at 14 he designed his first house. A graduate of the California Institute of Technology, he was the youngest person to pass the state architectural examinations and he scored the highest marks. Opening his practice in Pasadena, California he became an authority on earthquake construction but his specialty was church architecture. Hearing of the plan to build a cathedral in Washington, he followed the early planning and became acquainted with Bishop Harding. When Henry Vaughn died in 1917, Frohman submitted several designs and drawings that resulted in his firm's being appointed architects of the cathedral in 1920. He continued in this position until his death in 1972. Known as a genius in architecture, he may be said to have influenced the design of the cathedral to such an extent that it is his total design.

FRANK BILLINGS KELLOGG. Born December 22, 1856 in Potsdam, N. Y. His father joined the westward trend following the Civil War and moved to Minnesota in 1865. He had a very meager early education but still went to Rochester to read law. He was admitted to the bar in Minnesota in 1877. Because of the attention given some of his early litigation, he was recruited by the most prestigious law firm in Minnesota in 1887. Specializing in corporate law, he became intrigued with President Theodore Roosevelt's battle with the trusts and he joined the president. He took the lead in the cases against Standard Oil and subsequently became the chief counsel for the Interstate Commerce Commission. He was elected to the U. S. Senate from Minnesota in 1916. He was delegate to the Conference of American States in Chili, Ambassador to Great Britain and Secretary of State in 1925. He was one of the authors of the Kellogg-Briand Pact that renounced war as an instrument of national policy that was signed by 62 nations. He received the Nobel Peace Prize in 1929. Kellogg died in St. Paul, Minnesota in 1937.

BRECKINRIDGE LONG. b. May 16, 1881. d. September 26, 1958. Born in St. Louis, Missouri. A graduate of Princeton University in 1904, he was greatly influenced by his major professor, Woodrow Wilson. He studied law at Washington University and was admitted to the bar in 1906. He married a very wealthy woman in St. Louis who gave him freedom to follow his interest in politics. An Assistant Secretary of State, he resigned to run twice for the Senate only to be defeated. Appointed as Ambassador to Italy, he made amazingly accurate forecasts of war conditions in Europe. He resigned and returned to the States for surgery. During World War II, he was again appointed to the State Department as an Assistant Secretary.

JULIA GRANT CANTACUZENE. The granddaughter of President U. S. Grant, she was born in the White House in June 1876. Her father, Major General Frederick Dent Grant, was appointed Minister Plenipotentiary to Austria in 1889. Julia made her debut in Vienna and because of her personality and erudition in languages she became a favorite at the Royal court. In 1899 she met Prince Michael Cantacuzene of Russia and they were married later that year in Newport, Rhode Island. She lived in the family castles at Bouromka and in St. Petersburg. She fled Russia during the Revolution and later wrote three books of her memoirs, documenting the fate of the Russian aristocracy during the Revolution. She died in 1975.

WOODROW WILSON. Born in Staunton, Virginia on December 28, 1856 where his father was the Pastor of the First Presbyterian Church, he grew up in the south, in Savannah, Georgia; Columbia, South Carolina; and Wilmington, North Carolina. He graduated from Princeton University and received his doctorate in political economy from Johns Hopkins University with a brilliant dissertation on "Congressional Government." A distinguished member of the faculty at Princeton he was elected president of the university by its trustees in 1902. After his election as Governor of New Jersey in 1911,his progressive administration put him out front in the presidential election. He became the 28th President of the United States in 1912. He was re-elected to a second term in 1916. During World War I, the announcement of his Fourteen Points for securing the peace led directly to the armistice in November of that year. One of Wilson's 14 points was a proposal to establish the League of Nations. He suffered a stroke and was unable to give personal direction to a campaign for its acceptance. His writings and publications are extensive. He died in Washington on February 3, 1924.

All six of the former bishops of the Washington Diocese are also interred in the cathedral. To limit their introduction here as the diocesans, however, is to understate their involvement and influence in the cathedral. In every instance, the bishop served as the executive officer of the Cathedral Foundation. In some instances, he was also the dean. Among them, the bishops contributed to the iconography, raised funds for the construction, established policies to be observed on the close and guided those engaged in planning the building's future. They are listed in the order of their ordination, with the dates of their service in the diocese and the place of their interment.

THE RT. REV. HENRY YATES SATTERLEE 1896-1908
    Bethlehem Chapel

THE RT. REV. ALFRED HARDING 1909-1923
    Resurrection Chapel

THE RT. REV. JAMES EDWARD FREEMAN 1923-1943
St. Joseph's Chapel

THE RT. REV. ANGUS DUN 1944-1962
Bethlehem Chapel.

THE RT. REV. WILLIAM F. CREIGHTON 1962-1977
Bethlehem Chapel west aisle.

THE RT. REV. JOHN T. WALKER 1977-1989
Bethlehem Chapel west aisle.

It Took Two Centuries

From the very earliest days of the new Republic, the Founding Fathers spoke of the need to have a "Grand Church" in the nation's capital. There was no legislation that authorized such an edifice nor was there an Executive Directive from the President. But it was so well established in the minds of the early planners, it was taken for granted that such a church would be built in the fullness of time.

The site eventually selected for the Washington National Cathedral was not even considered by Major Pierre L'Enfant in 1791 when he was appointed to lay out a plan for the new capital city. It was much too far out in the country. Although it was almost the highest point above sea-level within the "ten miles square" that was to constitute the Nation's Capital, L'Enfant had decided on the proper site in his own mind, "The grand avenu [sic] connecting both the palace [White House] and the Federal House [Capitol] . . ." He foresaw several squares along this "avenu" that would accommodate the Judiciary Court, the National Bank, the playhouse, the market and exchange and the Grand Church.

Joseph Nourse had been appointed as the first Registrar of the Treasury during President Washington's first term. In 1813, Nourse purchased 57 acres of land that was at that time remote from the developed Washington City, and he named the hill Mount Alban, after his prior home in England. That name has persisted to this day, modified by the addition of "Saint" in later days.

Nourse built his home on this site. Although we have no information concerning the house he built, a large and ancient boxwood that is near to the present Church House is alleged to have been the gift of Thomas Jefferson to Nourse. Another boxwood in the same area is said to have grown from a sprig of boxwood in an inaugural bouquet worn by Dolley Madison.

In 1893, President Benjamin Harrison signed the Charter for the Protestant Episcopal Foundation that had previously been passed by Congress. This Charter has been called the "cathedral's birth certificate." With this authority to proceed, and with the backing of

Bishop Paret of the Diocese of Maryland, it took another five years to obtain land for the cathedral close. Finally, in 1898, The Right Reverend Henry Yates Satterlee, the first Bishop of the new Diocese of Washington, purchased a portion of the former Nourse estate.

With the site selected and the Cathedral Foundation chartered, planning for construction of the cathedral could now proceed. The timing associated with building the cathedral is indeed fascinating.

1791 - Formal planning for Washington City begins and is to include a "Grand Church."

1893 - President Harrison signs the Charter for the Foundation.

1990 - The completed cathedral is dedicated.

Future generations should mark their calendars for 2090. It would seem that something of significance is certain to occur at about that time.

The Coventry Cross of Nails

Gifts of art and artifacts have come to the cathedral from many different sources, but one that is unique is the Coventry Cross of Nails. A commemoration of the cathedral destroyed by bombing raids in 1940, it has been fashioned of 14th century nails that were used to support the roof beams of Coventry Cathedral.

The Cross of Nails has become an international symbol of reconciliation in that similar crosses have been distributed to persons and places on five continents. The cross given to Washington Cathedral was placed in the Mellon Bay, a lovely and private place for prayer and meditation. It is in the first bay, south outer aisle, west of the crossing. A wrought-iron gate has also been installed that gives the little chapel a feeling of seclusion.

Another Coventry Cross of Nails was given to the German people and hangs in the ruins of the Kaiser Wilhelm Church in Berlin where it commands great interest.

Completing the Nave

In the mid-1960s, it was decided to make a major effort to complete the construction of the nave in time for the Bicentennial celebration in 1976. At that time the cathedral was still using a general contractor, the George Fuller Company, a well known and reliable contractor who had worked at the cathedral for many years. The late Fred Maynard was the project superintendent and the officers of the company had impressed upon him the importance of meeting the date set for completing the nave.

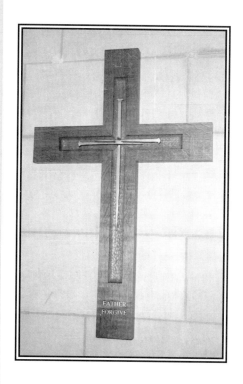

The Coventry Cathedral Cross of Nails.

In past years, if there had been one consistent factor that delayed the completion of any phase of work, it was the delivery of stone from the quarries in Indiana. One could always be certain that the stone would be late and that it might even be necessary to furlough some of the stone setting crews because of the delays. Selecting the area where he expected the most trouble, Maynard went to the limestone companies in Indiana and told them of his need for stone and for its timely delivery. When the quarry officials asked Maynard if he wanted one or two rail cars of stone a week, Maynard replied that he wanted the stone as fast as they could send it. He did not anticipate how the quarries might respond.

The first thing the quarries did was to increase their work force by a substantial number and to put their crews on over-time in order to produce the stone required "as fast as they could!" Very soon, Maynard was receiving at least one and sometimes two rail cars each day and he was forced to curtail the setting crews at the cathedral and to use all of his men just to unload the stone from the rail cars and to supervise its transfer to the construction site. He had to rent trucks to haul the stone up to Mt. St. Alban and he had to establish new stone yards to receive and hold the stone. When he tried to slow the quarries down, to deliver the stone on a more reasonable basis, they demurred since they had made commitments to their people and they kept them producing. Otto Epps recalls that the masons and mason helpers at the cathedral were frequently working as much in overtime as they worked in regular hours.

The nave was completed in time for the Bicentennial.

In the 1980s when the construction of the west towers was undertaken, Maynard had retired and was participating as a volunteer with the cathedral Construction Committee. This time he was careful to specify to the quarries the precise amounts of stone that he required and the dates by which he wanted it delivered. Alas, it was not to be! Once again, the stone was delivered late and, frequently, not in sequence.

Surveying the Completed Nave

When construction was resumed on the two west towers in 1983, there were concerns that by loading several hundred tons of stone on the west end each year, the tremendous weight might cause a compression of the west towers causing them to separate from the nave. If any such settlement were to be observed, then immediate action would need to be taken to counteract it.

The late Dr. Henry Lepper, a distinguished former professor of Civil Engineering at Yale University and the University of Maryland, agreed to meet with the staff at the cathedral and to devise a method to assure that no untoward twisting action in the cathedral structure was occurring. At his direction, small bronze pins were installed at a point on each of the major piers in the cathedral to serve as measuring points. With the help of a surveyer's transit and two volunteers, he did a complete survey of the nave floor that included the chapels. This survey was completed and checked to establish its validity and then used as a point of departure for succeeding surveys in each of several years following. On two occasions, the results of the transit survey were checked and measured against a new electronic distance measuring equipment that served to validate the results of the surveys. Following the untimely death of Dr. Lepper, the surveys were continued by Dr. Dennis McCahill until the construction was completed.

There was no evidence of any compression or settling of the west end. Although some very large cracks in the wall of the Rare Book Library did appear, these were considered to be related to other factors.

The Reverend Robert Hunt

As all school children can tell us, the first permanent English settlement in America was at Jamestown, Virginia in 1607. Departing from England on December 20, 1606, the *Sarah Constant*, the *Goodspeed* and the *Discovery*, 100 tons, 40 tons and 20 tons respectively, arrived at Jamestown Island on May 14, 1607, after 145 days at sea. The 120 men on board quickly set about establishing acceptable living conditions.

A member of the party, the Rev. Robert Hunt held the first Anglican religious service in the new world in very temporary facilities. The brick church was built later and portions of the church tower still stand on the island.

The Order of Jamestown arranged for a statue of the Rev. Robert Hunt to be presented to Washington National Cathedral. Accompanying the statue was a brick from the first church built at Jamestown. Both are installed in a niche over the south crypt aisle entrance to the Bethlehem Chapel. Since the chapel was the first part of the cathedral completed, it is appropriate that it should be the recipient of this gift from the first permanent settlement in America. The following citation accompanies the statue and brick:

THIS BRICK FROM THE CHURCH OF JAMESTOWN, VIRGINIA

A.D. 1607,

WAS PLACED AND HALLOWED BY THE BISHOP OF LONDON

ON BEHALF OF THE ORDER OF JAMESTOWN, OCTOBER 29,

A.D. 1926.

A brick from the first Anglican church at Jamestown, Virginia and statue commemorating the Rev. Robert Hunt.

"A House of Prayer for all People"

Of all the elements in the cathedral fabric, the Maryland Window probably best exemplifies the basic purpose for which the cathedral was constructed. The window is in the nave south aisle, the first bay east of the Washington Bay, installed in 1972 and designed by the artist, Rowan LeCompte. Consider what the three lancets say to us.

The left lancet portrays two of the early pioneers in America, Francis Asbury, the first Methodist bishop consecrated in America, and George Fox, founder of the Society of Friends.

✚ FRANCIS ASBURY was born near Birmingham, England in 1745. He converted to Methodism as a youth and became an itinerant preacher. He came to America as a missionary at the age of 26 when there were only about 300 Methodist converts and four ministers in the colonies. When most of the Methodists returned to England at the outbreak of war, he remained. Known as a constant and tireless traveler, he became the first bishop of the church in America and by 1816 he had brought the strength of the church to 214,000 members with some 2,000 ministers.

✚ GEORGE FOX was born in Leicestershire, England in 1624. He very soon gave himself up to a life of meditation and religious inquiry and in 1648 began a series of missionary journeys to spread his understanding of "the Light within," that had brought him such comfort. Because the Friends departed in their outward appearance and recognition of the accepted civilities of society, they were ostracized and Fox spent a large portion of his life in prison. He traveled to America in 1670 where he established the Society of Friends before his return to England in 1673.

The right lancet portrays the first Roman Catholic bishop in America, John Carroll and a sketch of Georgetown University which he founded. Below him, Father Andrew White is represented, the priest who celebrated the first Roman Catholic mass in America.

✚ JOHN CARROLL, born in 1735 at Upper Marlboro, Maryland was educated in France. He entered the Jesuit order in 1753 and was ordained a priest. He returned to America in 1774 and ministered to a congregation in Rock Creek. In 1776, he accompanied his cousin Charles Carroll and Benjamin Franklin on a diplomatic mission to Canada. He was consecrated a bishop in 1790 and in 1808 became the first Archbishop of Baltimore. He was active in establishing Roman Catholic educational institutions, including Georgetown University.

✚ THE REVEREND ANDREW WHITE, a Jesuit priest, embarked from England in November 1633 with a group of colonists aboard

The Ark and *The Dove*. This group, sponsored by Cecil Calvert, Lord Baltimore, arrived in the Chesapeake Bay and settled at St. Mary's City. On March 25, the first day of the new year, old style, mass was celebrated, the first Roman Catholic service to be conducted in America.

Father White wrote the *Relatio Itineris* that has survived as the most authoritative account of the early life of settlers in Maryland. He agreed with Lord Baltimore that the colony should be based on religious liberty and labored to this end. Alas, it was not to be. In 1646, Captain Richard Ingle, an English parliamentarian, clamped the 66-year-old Father White in chains and took him back to England. Once released in England he asked to be returned to his Maryland, but his age and infirmities would not allow it. He died in England in 1656 at the age of 76.

The center lancet shows the first Episcopal bishop consecrated in America, Thomas John Claggett. Below him is a characterization of Captain John Smith, normally associated with Virginia, but a man who diligently explored the Chesapeake Bay and the rivers emptying into the bay. At the bottom of the three lancets one can see pictured fish and flowers associated with Maryland, and, of course, a Baltimore oriole.

✦ Thomas John Claggett became the first Episcopal bishop to be consecrated in America. Born in Prince George's County Maryland, he went first to Princeton and from there to London where he was ordained a deacon in 1764. Returning to Maryland, he served several parishes including St. Anne's in Annapolis and St. Paul's in Prince George's County. In 1792 he was elected bishop, just 100 years after passage of the act establishing the Episcopal Church in Maryland.

In 1800 he was appointed Chaplain of the United States Senate and some years afterward founded Trinity Church at Upper Marlboro, Maryland. He spent his later years at Croome, one of the original tracts of land patented to his grandfather Captain Thomas Claggett and transmitted to his descendants. He died in August 1816 and was interred in a family lot, his grave marked by a marble slab with a eulogy written by Francis Scott Key. His remains were later removed and reinterred in Washington National Cathedral.

✦ JOHN SMITH, born in Lincolnshire, England, became a soldier of fortune at an early age. He served with the Huguenots in France before drifting to eastern Europe to oppose the Turks. He sailed with the first expedition of the London Company intent on establishing colonies in America. Smith was a very controversial person. Though he was credited with securing corn from the Indians and thus saving the colonists from starvation, he was both pilloried and praised for his accomplishments. Smith explored the Chesapeake Bay and its tributary rivers and made very usable early maps of the Bay. He subsequently explored New England and wrote a somewhat fanciful history of his experiences.

The quatrefoil for the window commemorates the Act of Toleration, passed by the Maryland General Assembly in 1649. This was the first instance of a legal act that made it possible for persons of different religious persuasions to live together in peace.

It is most appropriate to commemorate these persons and the Act of Toleration in "A House of Prayer for all People."

The Larz Anderson Tapestries

For centuries it has been customary in many countries for the populace to contribute gifts of great value to cathedrals. In Europe, many of the cathedrals maintain treasuries where valuable gifts of gemstones, silver or gold are kept. On occasion, these treasuries are displayed for view by the public, but typically they are under lock and key.

Ambassador and Mrs. Larz Anderson gave the funds for St. Mary's Chapel in Washington Cathedral. The polychromed reredos made of linden wood and carved by the artist Ernest Pelligrini, follows the medieval custom of showing the two donors in kneeling profile at the base corners. Both of the donors are interred in the carved tomb on the north wall of the chapel.

Following the death of her husband, Mrs. Anderson gave the six tapestries to the cathedral with the request that they hang in St. Mary's Chapel. Woven during the latter half of the 16th Century in Brussels, when that city was known as a center for tapestry weaving, they tell the story of David and Goliath and of the enmity that existed between David and King Saul. Unlike many of the sets of tapestries woven in Brussels, this set enjoyed only three owners. The first was the Count Flaminio Mannelli, secretary to Cardinal d'Este, Papal Legate at the Court of King Charles IX of France. D'Este, leader of the Italian house by that name, presented the tapestries to Mannelli as a token of his esteem and in recognition of his services not only to him, but to his Queen, Catherine de Medici, then Dowager Queen of France. Mannelli hung them in his palace in 1587 and there they remained until 1898 when the Larz Andersons purchased them from their second owner, the Marquis Pianetti of Jesi. Brought to America, they decorated the walls of the Anderson mansion on Massachusetts Avenue until Mr. Anderson's death in April 1937. Six months later his widow, knowing her husband's wishes in the matter, bequeathed them to the cathedral. [1]

Each of the panels, which are almost perfectly preserved, measures approximately 11.5-feet square.

---

[1]   Elizabeth Oldfield, "The Larz Anderson Tapestries," *The Cathedral Age*, Winter 1946

Bells in the Old Post Office

The story begins in London.

The students of the National Cathedral School Whitechapel Guild were on tour in England in 1976 and visited the Whitechapel Foundry, the foundry that cast and installed the peal bells in the cathedral's central tower. In walking through the foundry yard, their leader, Rick Dirksen, saw a set of bells that were engraved "Washington, D.C." His curiosity was piqued. For whom were they intended? Where were they to go? How were they to be installed? The Foundry Official was reticent to discuss the matter and told Rick that the whole subject was confidential. Upon being pressed, the official suggested that some information might be obtained from the United States Congress but that he was unable to disclose anything further.

The story moves to Washington.

Upon his return to this country, Rick called on a friend who was a member of Congress. The congressman knew nothing about the matter, but he was persuaded to investigate. Over a period of time, parts of the story began to emerge. At first these bits of unrelated data formed a rather unfocused collage. As more information became available, however, the collage grew to become a remarkable work of art.

The story moves back to England.

There is in England a well known philanthropic foundation known as Ditchley. It takes its name from a very lovely country estate in the mid-lands where visiting heads of state have met from time to time to consider weighty issues. On occasion during World War II, Winston Churchill would spend a weekend at Ditchley rather than at the Prime Minister's country estate at Chequers since Ditchley was believed not to be known to the Luftwaffe and was not as likely to be targeted in an air raid.

With the approaching celebration of the American Bicentennial in 1976, the officials at Ditchley thought it would be a very timely and appropriate observance of the occasion for the British Parliament to tender a gift of peal bells to the United States Congress, with the bells to be installed in the United States Capitol. Ditchley had the bells cast, but Parliament subsequently determined to make a different gift. So Ditchley proffered the gift to the Congress themselves.

The story returns to Washington.

Members of Congress knew quite well that there was no place in the Capitol building where peal bells might be installed. What were they to do? It was undiplomatic as well as impolitic, not to mention impolite, to refuse a gift that had been proffered. But if Congress accepted the bells, there would be an obligation to provide a bell tower where they might be installed. This raised problems that were difficult to comprehend. The problems were even more difficult to resolve. Congress delayed action; Congress is quite skilled at that.

There is no record of any ill tempers manifesting themselves. But there was a concern at the Whitechapel Foundry about the bells. The bells had been paid for by Ditchley but what was to become of them? The men at Ditchley, in Parliament, in Congress, and at the Whitechapel Foundry were unable to resolve this dilemma. It took a woman's touch!

Nancy Hanks, Chairman of the National Endowment for the Arts, headed the committee concerned with renovating the Old Post Office building on Pennsylvania Avenue. Once the dilemma of the bells found its way to her attention, significant changes were made for the Tower of the Old Post Office building that enabled the Old Post Office to receive the peal. The bells were then accepted by Congress, and the installation was completed.

But that is not the end of the story.

There was no one in the City of Washington administration who could ring a bell peal. No one in Congress knew how to ring a bell peal. The only trained and competent bell ringers were at Washington National Cathedral. They have been ringing peals in the Old Post Office building ever since.

That is the end of the story.

The Masonic Cathedral Builders

People enjoy building and the experience of creating that accompanies it. This is especially obvious when they are working to build something very special. Speak to those who have been associated with the construction of Washington Cathedral, and they will assure you that it is so.

This fact was documented in 1925 in an article published in The Master Mason [2] in January of that year. Two men were mentioned in the article.

Charles Austin worked at the cathedral as a stone cutter and mason. He was popular with the other workmen at the cathedral and had expressed his feelings about the privilege of working there in rather eloquent terms. Austin, who was a member of the Blue Lodge, died late in 1924. "I have often wondered," he said, "at the devotion shown by the workmen on Solomon's Temple, the consecration to their task of the cathedral builders of the Middle Ages and the inspiration which the people of their time received from these witnesses to God, and I believe I have begun to understand it, to feel it as I have watched this building grow day by day."

On the occasion of his death, all work at the cathedral stopped for one hour. His spirit, it was said, had permeated the construction community.

The second person was named Robert F. Biel, a transient worker who appeared on the site and showed a pin that he wore marked

2   Oliver Hoyem, "Masonry and Cathedral Building," The Master Mason, Volume II, Number 1, January 1, 1925.

'Temple Builder." The pin signified that he had given one hundred dollars toward the construction of the Masonic Temple in Washington a very significant sum in those days.

Biel said he had no family and he had no money to spare but he wanted to contribute to the construction of the cathedral. He worked as a laborer for one month and donated all of the money he earned to the building fund of the cathedral. He was described as an excellent worker.

Memorial Service for Fred Maynard

It was in January 1987 that a memorial service was held at the cathedral for Fred Maynard. He had been a Chief Engineer for the Fuller Construction Company and for many years he had been the principal supervisor for the construction at the cathedral. After he had retired, he came back to the cathedral as a volunteer and served as a member of the Construction Committee. Committee members would tease Fred about his estimates of the cost of construction. They were so accurate that he was jokingly accused of using black magic to obtain them.

Fred was a pipe smoker and when he came to the meetings of the Construction Committee, he would invariably have a tobacco pouch and two or more pipes that would see him through the meeting. He always sat at one end of the table, away from the non-smokers, where he was joined by the author who was another pipe smoker at that time. In the early 1980s the Committee was meeting in one of the rooms on the second level of the northwest tower. The two pipe smokers were both embarrassed when cathedral Security interrupted the meeting to see if there was a fire in the room.

Fred loved to bowl and to play golf. In his last several years he took the opportunity to enjoy both. During the season, Fred played golf weekly with friends of his and it was one such occasion that led tragically to his death. After the game, Fred was removing his clubs from the golf cart to put them in his car, when his friend accidentally put the transmission of the golf cart in reverse; Fred was knocked to the ground and lapsed into a coma from which he never recovered.

Fred's two sons were here for the memorial service. They were deeply touched to witness the respect and affection that all of the cathedral workmen and staff held for their father.

Cathedral Builders

There are also those who carve no statues, set no stones nor design any of the artistic embellishments to the cathedral, but who provide the funds and the guidance that make it possible for others to do so. It would not be imaginable that the many contributors over a period of 83 years who gave money to the construction of the cathedral could be listed here. There are two families, however, who have made such continuous and substantial contributions and who had such a lasting impact on the cathedral that it would be inappropriate not to acknowledge them.

The White-Bennett Families.

. . . The Honorable Henry White and his wife, Margaret Stuyvesant Rutherfurd White. Mr. White served as a member of the Cathedral Foundation Chapter from 1915 until his death in 1927. A distinguished diplomat, he had served as Ambassador to Italy and later to France. He was a delegate to the Versailles Peace Conference at the close of World War I. He was also a member of the Cathedral Building Committee, a member of the Board of the National Cathedral School for Girls and chairman of the New York Committee of the National Cathedral Association. An outer aisle bay on the north side of the nave has been given as a memorial to Mr. and Mrs. Henry White. The second Mrs. Henry White (Emily Vanderbilt Sloane) provided the funds for the great west rose window, a gift to memorialize her sons.

. . . A second generation was represented by their son, John Campbell White and his wife, Elizabeth, of Easton, Maryland. They also were benefactors of the cathedral and they continued the tradition of service. It was Mrs. John Campbell White who was instrumental in beginning the idea of hostesses to greet guests and visitors, the forerunners of the present Cathedral Guides. Primarily instrumental in the dedication of the northwest tower pinnacle to the memory of Henry White, she thought it appropriate that "since he was in on the beginning he should be in at the end."

. . . The third generation in this family is represented by Margaret White Bennett and her late husband, the Honorable W. Tapley Bennett, Jr. Mrs. Bennett has served several terms on the Cathedral Building Committee.

. . . Commander and Mrs. John C.W. Bennett and Mr. William T. Bennett, III represent the fourth generation of the family in active support of the cathedral.

It was appropriate that one day before the final stone was set on the cathedral, a ceremony marked the gift of the great pinnacle on the northwest tower to the memory of Henry White and three generations of his descendants.

The Glover Families.

. . . Charles Carroll Glover, a man of unusual vision, came to Washington as a youth of 19 and remained until his death 71 years later. For all of this time, he was associated with Riggs Bank, and for most of those years he was its president. As much as any man, he was responsible for the development of Rock Creek Park as a recreational center for the District of Columbia. He hosted the first meeting of a group of public spirited persons in his home in 1891, to discuss the possibility of building a cathedral in the nation's capital. It was shortly after that meeting that the Diocese of Washington was created and that active work began towards the creation of the Protestant Episcopal Cathedral Foundation.

. . . Mr. Glover served as a member of the Board of Trustees and later a member of the Cathedral Foundation Chapter for many years. At his funeral, the Bishop of Washington referred to him as one of his most outstanding and conspicuous aides.

. . . Charles Carroll Glover, Jr. followed in his father's footsteps and became a director of Riggs Bank and, in 1948, a member of the Cathedral Foundation Chapter. He was also very active in the community, serving on the boards of many charities and eleemosynary institutions. He served continuously as a member of the Foundation Chapter until his retirement in the late 1960s.

. . . Charles Carroll Glover III, had the unusual privilege of succeeding to his father's position on the Foundation Chapter when his father retired. Active as a lawyer on the Washington scene, he was selected as the Junior Chamber of Commerce "Young Man of the Year" in 1954, served as Chairman of the Eugene and Agnes Meyer Foundation Board of Directors and was a Director of the Riggs Bank for many years. Charles Glover served on the Foundation Chapter until the mid-1970s.

. . . Virginia Dougherty Glover, (Mrs. Charles Carroll Glover III) was appointed to the Chapter in 1978. She too was active in opportunities for service, having been Chairman of the Board of Trustees of Smith College and later president of the National Cathedral Association. She was Chairman of the Cathedral's Development Campaign from 1986 to 1992 and she has also served as a member of the Cathedral Building Committee.

Certainly, four members of the Cathedral Foundation Chapter all in one family is unique. Their contribution to the cathedral governance and its development has been significant. The Glover Bay on the south side of the nave that contains, appropriately, the Founder's Window, memorializes the Glover family.

The Tenacity of St. Joan of Arc

History records that St. Joan of Arc commanded the French army that relieved the siege of Orleans and led subsequently to the defeat of the English. But all of that occurred back in the 15th century. Is it possible that the spirit of this tenacious and relentless maiden was still active in World War II?

There is a special stained-glass window of St. Joan at Washington National Cathedral on the north side of the nave, the first bay west of the crossing. The window was commissioned to Wilbur H. Burnham and it was completed in 1942. Mr. Burnham ordered some of the stained glass from an English factory that was shipped early in 1941, but the ship was torpedoed. The captain managed to save some of his cargo which included the crate of stained glass and it was shipped again on another vessel later in the year. Strangely, though, the second ship was also torpedoed. Again the crate of glass was saved and eventually it arrived at its destination. The glass was intact. A poster had been tacked to the crate which read, "England Delivers the Goods!" [3]   Well, the English certainly did their part in delivering the stained glass, but it seems most obvious that the spirit of a very precocious, pertinacious, persevering young maiden must have made it all happen.

Special Memorial Stones

From the earliest days of construction, gift stones of symbolic or memorial significance have been received and have been used in the construction of either the cathedral or the embellishment of the Bishop's Garden. In the latter instance, most of the special stones were actively acquired by the cathedral family. Those in the cathedral have all been gifts.

In the northwest porch stairway to the lower level of the cathedral, there are a series of interesting stones set in the wall. Each of the stones offers just enough information to invite one's curiosity. Each has a story to tell.

1.   On the top stairway landing, a dark stone in the wall bears the notation, "ST. DAVID'S WALES"

The stone, taken from the ancient fabric of St. David's Cathedral in Wales, was presented to the cathedral by the St. David's Society of Washington, D. C. on Sunday, February 27, 1955.

---

3   *The Cathedral Age,* Winter 1941

At the first landing:

2. "TO ANTHONY SHANDS WHOSE LABOR HELPED BUILD WASHINGTON CATHEDRAL, WITH APPRECIATION FROM THE DEAN, NOVEMBER 1964"

Anthony Shands was a model laborer. He could be counted on always to be present, always to be positive, always to be constant. It would have been most inappropriate not to have commemorated his service.

3. "TO JAMES SMITH, LIKE HIS LORD A CARPENTER AND BUILDER OF THIS CATHEDRAL, BY THE DEAN, NOVEMBER 1971"

James Smith came to the cathedral as a carpenter in 1946, following World War II. Known as "Jimmy" to the cathedral staff, he worked continuously and diligently. A carpenter foreman, he was skilled at translating the architects' drawings into the templates required for construction. He was forced to retire because of illness. He died while instructing his replacement.

4. AN ORNAMENTAL STONE OF HERALDRY. IT CONTAINS A SHIELD, A KNIGHT'S HELMET, WITH A LANCE AND EAGLE SUPERIMPOSED, A STAR AND OTHER DECORATIONS.

Unlike the other stones, the giver as well as the purpose of this gift have been lost.

5. "TO HENRY QUOTON, WHOSE LABOR HELPED BUILD WASHINGTON CATHEDRAL WITH APPRECIATION FROM THE DEAN, NOVEMBER 1964"

Henry Quoton was a laborer, employed by the George Fuller Company, who worked at many of the support jobs associated with the construction. Primarily, he was a mason's helper who mixed mortar. Jack Fanfani recalls when he was a very small lad, his father would slip Quoton a quarter to let little Jack play in the sand pile while he mixed mortar.

Along the lower stairs:

6. A dark stone, "ALOHA FROM THE CHURCH SCHOOLS OF HAWAII"

A gift to Washington Cathedral from the St. Andrew's Priory School for Girls and the Iolani School for Boys, St. Andrew's Cathedral, Honolulu.

163

7. STONE FROM MT. SINAI

A stone from the Chapel of Moses on Mt. Sinai. This is one of several, the others having been incorporated in the floor before the High Altar so that, in Washington Cathedral, the Ten Commandments may be read from a place that is intimately associated with the beginning of Mosaic Law.

8. "FIRST CENTURY STONE FRAGMENT FROM ALONG THE APPIAN WAY (QUEEN OF ROADS) LEADING INTO ROME"

A stone from a tomb on the Appian Way presented by St. Paul's Church in Rome

9. GITMO (Acronym for Guantanamo Bay, Cuba)

The Commanding Officer of Guantanamo Naval Base presented a stone to the cathedral as a memento of Dean Francis Sayre's visit to Guantanamo in the summer of 1964. When this stone was first set, it had a polished face that shone as if it were a beacon to attract one's attention. After the brightness was burnished away it blended more closely with the surrounding limestone ashlars.

In the Bishop's Garden one can find interesting and more ancient stones. Most of these were installed in accordance with designs prepared by Florence Bratenahl, garden designer.

An old English sundial on a 700-year-old French capital found in monastic ruins near Rheims, France.

10. A 12th century Norman arch and a 15th century bas-relief of the Crucifixion, the Virgin Mary and St. John. This collection of several stones was brought from France and incorporated in a charming small Norman Court with fountain.

11. A 9th century Carolingian baptismal font. This has been surrounded with plant materials similar to those used at the same time, according to Charlemagne's plant list of 812 A.D.

12. An old English sundial that rests atop a 13th century Gothic capital. The capital was discovered in monastic ruins near Rheims Cathedral in France.

13. A Wayside Cross. Inscribed with the sacred monogram for Jesus, and dating from early Christian pilgrimages, the cross is installed along with two 15th century bas-reliefs of saints and martyrs.

14. A 15th century bas-relief of St. Catherine. Installed near a small pool designed in the shape of a primitive cross.

15. The Prodigal Son. Although it is contemporary, this sculpture by Heinz Warneke, is a focal point in the garden and is an appropriate addition.

The Prodigal Son.
Sculpture by Heinz Warneke.

Volunteers at
Washington National Cathedral

One is drawn to consider the similarities between Washington National Cathedral and the many great cathedrals in England that were built in earlier centuries. There is one distinct difference. At Washington a host of volunteers serve in a wide variety of activities. According to Barbara D. Dewey, the former Coordinator of Volunteers, more than 800 are actively involved.

In a report prepared by Dewey on this phase of the cathedral's life, she says:

"Our cathedral family of volunteers includes persons of many faiths, ages, cultural backgrounds, race experiences and professions.

Some are Lutherans, Roman Catholic, Methodists, Episcopalians, Jews, Presbyterians, as well as other faiths, while some are still seeking their faith tradition. They are young, middle-aged and old; they are former teachers, secretaries, home-makers, lawyers, engineers, organists, foreign-service officers. And what binds this wonderfully diversified group together is their love of the National Cathedral.

"Cathedral volunteers do many jobs; they perform many services for the cathedral. In fact, there are over 40 different ways in which a person can minister at the cathedral. They welcome the thousands of visitors from all over our country and the world and make them feel at home here; they give tours both general and specialized. They work with children in the Medieval Workshop, helping them to learn the crafts needed to build a Gothic cathedral.

"Some serve in the cathedral shops, helping with customers or behind the scenes. Others help as assistants in the various offices on the close.

"Another vital area in which many volunteers are involved is in community outreach. For example they serve at Martha's Table (a "soup" kitchen which helps to feed the hungry) and SOME (So Others Might Eat). Over 200 currently tutor children in the District of Columbia schools in reading and math and also adults who need assistance with their reading.

"An area of volunteer service is with the Worship Department. Many dedicated volunteers usher at the many services, serve on the Altar Guild or act as Lay Readers and Chalice Bearers. The Nave Clergy Program is made up of volunteer clergy who give one day a week to assist with services and to counsel to visitors and staff.

"Then there are those wonderful happy bell ringers, those who do archival work, those who are computer specialists in the offices and those who graciously serve behind the scene in so many ways and for so many special cathedral programs. And quite a few committed souls serve on the various boards, such as the Cathedral Chapter, the Building Committee, Washington Committee of the National Cathedral Association, All Hallows Guild, all giving their time, wisdom and support so willingly."

People tend not to volunteer unless they feel a large measure of fulfillment and satisfaction in what they do. It is only necessary to observe the volunteers at the cathedral to know that they consider themselves to be richly rewarded.

The construction of the cathedral has been completed. The opportunities for service continue.

The Unique Function
and Role of a National Cathedral

A national cathedral is a very special place. It is a place where a nation's people go to celebrate and share great joy. It is a place where they go to seek solace in times of sorrow and sadness. It is a place to memorialize great achievements. It is a place to go in thanksgiving and with gratitude for rich blessings.

But a national cathedral is more than a place; it is an institution. Its constitution is of flesh and blood as much as it is of stone and mortar. It becomes a nation's journal that documents the time in which it was built, and yet it is timeless. This cathedral stands on the highest elevation in the city seeking always to elevate the Nation's vision, yet acknowledging its myopia. For a thousand different individuals it stands for a thousand different things, and all of them can be compatible.

I have been associated with construction projects for over 40 years. Construction is always an uplifting experience, morale is high, there is a natural excitement about creating; people like to build. But nowhere have I experienced the atmosphere, the attitudes, the sense of commitment that existed at the Washington Cathedral.

Every fall, in November or December, we had to stop construction for the winter. The masons, the laborers, the tradesmen left and sought other employment. Every spring, in March or April, our construction period would begin again. And always the same people would appear! They came back. No matter what they had been doing, they came back. They would leave the other employment and return to the cathedral. It was not just a job, it was a commitment. It was not just a responsibility, it was an obsession!

And there is another observation; there was only one way to do the work at the cathedral. It had to be perfect. "Good enough" was not acceptable. No matter what the task, it was never necessary to ask, there was only one way to accomplish it. Perfection was the only standard; and the workmen were grateful for the privilege to be there. It was endemic for everyone on the job.

It has frequently been noted that there are two principal hills in Washington. One is Capitol Hill which symbolizes for our Nation the great instruments of our democracy, the Declaration of Independence and the Constitution. The other hill is Mt. St. Alban, where reposes the root document that underlies those instruments of democracy, *the original copy of the King James translation of the Bible*. It is from the faith embodied in the Bible that freedom and democracy grow. On both the hills, the same issues need addressing, and while the government wrestles with them from a political sense, those at the cathedral must consider them from a moral sense. It is proper that the two hills should be separate. It is also proper that they should each have the other in view.

In a brief publication issued by the Washington National Cathedral in 1976, this prayer composed by Dean Sayre was included:

"O THOU AUTHOR OF ALL MAJESTY,

WHO FIRST DIDST MAKE US OF THE CLAY,

THEN GAVE IT TO OUR HAND

THAT WE TOO MIGHT MAKERS BE;

GUIDE OUR FINGER IN THE SAND,

AFTER THEE TO TRACE THE GLORY

UNTIL THY HOUSE IS BUILT

THY FREEDOM SEEN

AND THY SERVANTS BLESSED

WHO LIFT THEIR LIVES TO THEE."

What more is there to say,
but Amen?

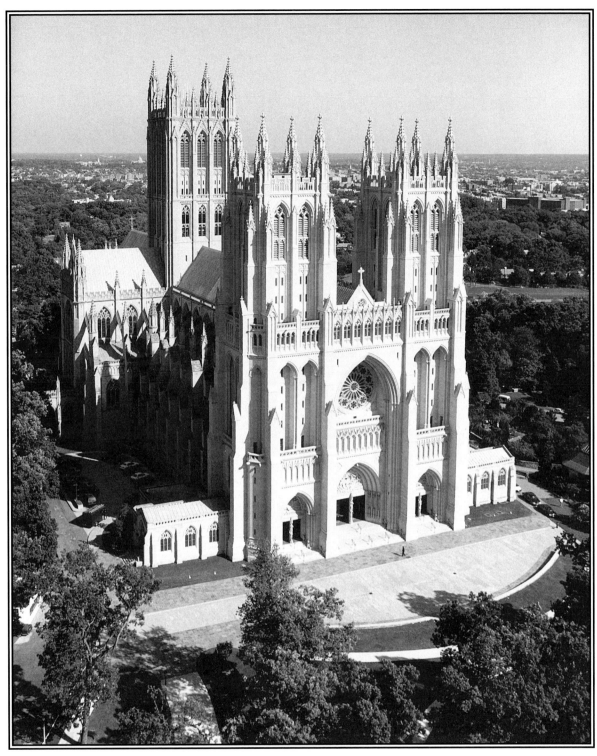

Photograph by Robert C. Lautman

Acknowledgments

I would be remiss if I did not acknowledge the early encouragement of my colleagues at Ingraham Planning Associates, Inc., Bob Ingraham, Vic Evans, Judy Chalfont, Colleen Walacavage, John Young. It was largely they who got me started. Dr. Richard Hewlett, Historiographer of the cathedral has helped to authenticate many of the items. Margaret Lewis and Jesse Wilson have helped to locate many items in the Cathedral Archives. Richard S. Dirksen, Barbara Dewey, Jack Fanfani, Jan Delberto, Carrie Kornick, Constantine Seferlis and Otto Epps have provided very important continuity as well as verification of some items that were otherwise in question. Nancy Montgomery, the long-time editor of *Cathedral Age*, has patiently corrected many false understandings that I entertained. I am grateful to Dodge Thompson, a colleague on the Cathedral Building Committee, who contributed the Foreword. Thomas S. Huestis, the art consultant, was given only flesh and bones but transformed it to a *corpus* that lives and breathes. A very gracious lady, Evelyn P. Metzger, has been both final editor and Publisher and has tempered my tendency to self-destruct. My son-in-law, T. Tilghman Herring, Jr. AIA, provided the art work for the frontispiece. My daughters, Karen Doubek and Margaret Herring both turned the tables by giving their father some important and timely advice. He listened. Finally, my wife Jeanne has been encouraging, exacting, and, thank heavens, forgiving!

Glossary

For the convenience of those unfamiliar with certain architectural terms that apply typically to cathedrals only, this glossary has been appended. The precise definition of the term has been altered, in some instances, so that it describes its relationship to Washington National Cathedral only.

Apse   The eastern termination of the sanctuary of a cathedral. Usually round or polygonal in shape.

Boss   A projecting stone at the intersection of ribs in the vaulting. Frequently called a keystone. Typically, the boss is carved elaborately as a part of the embellishment of the facility.

Buttress   A rectangular column of masonry, either free standing or attached to the exterior wall of a church, designed to counteract the lateral thrust of vaults or wind loads.

Canopy   A protective cover or roof over a sculpture.

Cathedra   The chair or throne of a bishop.

Clerestory   A wall, or story, that rises above a roof, is pierced by windows and that serves to light the interior by natural means. The clerestory windows at Washington National Cathedral are the largest windows in the edifice.

Close   The ground area on which the cathedral, schools and all of the supporting buildings stand. It also includes all roadways, play fields and gardens.

Columbarium   That portion of the crypts that contain recesses for urns or caskets.

Corbel   A stone that projects beyond the face of the wall in which it is set in order to give support to a vaulting rib or other structural member. It is usually carved.

Crocket   An ornamental and sculptured projecting piece of stone used to decorate sloping surfaces of pinnacles or gablets.

Drip Mould   A projecting piece of stone, usually over a window or arch, designed to throw off rain and prevent it from staining walls. The termination of a drip mould is usually carved, in foliage, a head, a small animal or a grotesque.

Finial   The topmost portion of a pinnacle. A vertical member usually decorated with crockets or other carving.

Gargoyle   A pierced stone projecting from the building, designed to carry water away from the building and its foundations. Usually carved to resemble a beast or mythical creature.

Iconography   The symbolic representation of holy scripture, in stone carvings, stained glass, wrought iron or other materials in the cathedral.

Lancet   A pointed, arched opening in a window, usually strong vertical members, and usually arranged in groups of two to four per window.

Nave   The main body of a church, where the congregation is seated, extending from the west front to the crossing. Usually flanked by an aisle on each side, much narrower and lower than the nave.

Niche   A recess in the face of a wall, prepared for a statue.

Pier   A mass of masonry, usually a cluster of columns, designed to support an arch or a vault.

Pinnacle   The upright structures representing the highest points of the three towers at the cathedral. There are four major pinnacles on each tower with other smaller intervening pinnacles.

Reredos   A screen or decorated wall behind an altar.

Rib   One of the visual stone arches, extending from the tops of piers to the bosses, that divide the vault into separate compartments.

Tracery   The ornate stone mullions in stained-glass windows.

Transept   The north and south wings of the cathedral that intersect the nave at the great crossing. The plan form of the transepts with the nave and choir form a cross.

Triforium   The middle level of the three level vertical interior wall at the cathedral. It is the gallery over the sloping roof over the side aisles.

Trumeau   A column in the center of two adjoining doors that support the tympanum above.

Tympanum   The space above a portal and within the arch above. Usually decorated with very rich sculpture.

Verge   A staff, similar to a mace, carried as a symbol of authority in a procession.

Verger   An official who carries the verge in a procession and goes before the bishop, clergy or other participants in religious service. He determines the order of the service as well as the responsibility of other participants.

Vaulting   A masonry ceiling based on the arch principle, the stones of which sustain themselves within the ribs.

Index

Administration Building, 110

All Hallows Guild, Founded by Mrs. Florence
Bratenahl, 147
    Tea and Tour program, 92

Ambry Door, ashes in the Ambry, 104
    designing, 59

Amish visitors, 81

Ancient Society of College Youths, 143

Anderson, Larz, tapestries, 156

Asbury, Bishop Francis, 154

Auditorium, 65

Austin, Charles, 158

Baez, Joan, 90

Baptismal Font, Resurrection Chapel, 126
    south transept, 63

Bagpipes, 73

Barnes, Ronald, 74

Bayless, John, bio, 102-117

Bells in the Old Post Office, 157

Bennett Family, 160

Bernstein, Leonard, 34

Biel, Robert F., 158

Bodley, Dr. George, 57

Bossanyi, Ervin, visit by Dirksen, 75
    visit from helper, 81

Bratenahl, Dr. George C. F., house, 106
    interment, 147

Bratenahl, Florence B., Herb Cottage, 140
    interment, 147

Bredlow, Tom, 133

Bulgarian Women, 81

Burnham, Wilbur H., 162

Bush, Carl, one of eight heads, 115

Callaway, Paul, Choirmaster, 69
    one of eight heads, 115
    playing the harpsichord, 129
    with the Pipers, 73

Canopy for the Majestus, 136

Cantacuzene, Julia Grant, 148

Carpenter, Jay, 82

Carroll, Bishop John, 154

Chavez, Cesar, 25

Chilcott, John, 143

Claggett, Rt. Rev. Thomas John, 155

Cleland, Peter "Billy", bio. 118-123

Competition for a gargoyle, 31

Coventry Cross of Nails, 151

Cram, Ralph Adams, Te Deum windows, 57
    Wilson canopy, 49

Creighton, Rt. Rev. William F., 150

Dalai Lama, 85

Daniels, Margaret Truman, 88

DeMazaire, Prime Minsiter, 83

Dewey, Admiral George, 147

Dewey, Barbara D., 165

Dill, Sir John, 40

Dirksen, Richard Wayne, bio, 69-79
    Old Post Office bells, 157
    portable organ, 45
    public address systems, 53
    Rick Dirksen, changing socks, 129
    Ringing Master, 144

Ditchley, 157

Doubek, Robert W., 145

Dun, Rt. Rev. Angus, interment, 150
    Seminary professor, 13

duPont sisters, 55

Eight heads on a buttress, 115

Eisenhower, President D. D., funeral, 17
    Sayre meeting with, 14

Epps, Otto, completing nave, 151
    "Laurel and Hardy", 144

Ethnic Angels, 18

Evans, Rev. Theodore H., 145

Ewan, Alec, 119

Fanfani, Italo, 104

Fanfani, Jack, ashes in Ambry, 105
    both labor and management, 114
    golfing, 78

Feller, Richard T., bio, 36-68
    gargoyle competition, 31
    radiant heating, 137
    Tucker's evaluation, 139
    visit to Taylor Foundry, 74

Fox, Rev. George, 154

Freeman, Rt. Rev. James E., economist, 113
    interment, 149
    woman driver, 88

Frohman, Philip Hubert, bearing, 134
    building the Tower, 45
    changing the vaulting, 47
    designing library, 44
    eight heads, 115
    Frohman-Warneke argument, 38
    harpsichord, 129
    interment, 147
    Majestus canopy, 136
    Morigi's opinion, 99
    public address systems, 53
    "Scotch" Gothic, 131
    selecting light fixtures, 42
    silver hat, 134
    small house plans, 111
    Te Deum windows, 57
    transept entrance ceilings, 127
    Tucker's evaluation, 139
    vaulting compression, 21

Gandhi, Mahatma, 26
Garagiola, Joe, 89
Gargoyle, the last, 82
Garner, The Rev. Sanford, 90
Garth Fountain, 55
Glastonbury, Cathedra, 29
Glover Family, 160
Goldkuhle, Dieter, 61
Guantanamo Bay, Cuba, 164
Guarenti, John, 56

Haines, Rt. Rev. Ronald, 90
Hancock, Walker, Lincoln statue, 66
    Majestus sculptor, 59
Hanks, Nancy, 157
Harding, Rt. Rev. Alfred, 149
Harpsichord, 129
Harrison, President Benjamin, 151
Hart, Frederick, Adam sculpture, 25
    a stone carver, 97
    St. Paul statue, 141
Haseltine, Herbert, 40
Henn, Herr Ulrich, 142
Herb Cottage, 140
Houghton, Arthur, 20
Hull, Secretary Cordell, 147
Hunt, Rev. Robert, 153

Immigration Service, 113

Kagawa, Toyohiko, daughter of, 83
Kaiser, Howard, 43
Keller, Helen, corbel, 131
    plaque for, 145
Kellogg, Frank Billings, 148
Kibbey, Bessie J., 73
King, Olive, 54
Kraus, John, 76

LeCompt, Irene and Rowan, 22
LeCompt, Rowan, Apse windows, 61
    Maryland window, 154
Lee, Katharine, her dog, 29
    Whitechapel Guild of Bell Ringers, 143
L'Enfant, Major Pierre, 150
Lepper, Dr. Henry, 152
Lincoln, Abraham, Hancock statue, 142
    Houck sculpture, 84
Linden crane, 46
Linkletter, Art, 89
Long, Breckinridge, 148
Lualdi, Angelo, 142

McCarthy, Senator Joseph, 30
Majestus, canopy, 136
    sculpting, 59
Maynard, Fred, completing nave, 151
    memorial service, 159
Miller, Jane K. L., bio, 80-92
Monjo, Enrique, 49
Monks, Canon G. Gardner, 39
Moon Rock, 23
Morigi, Roger, bio, 93-101
    caricature, 56
    carving Ishmael, 105
    carving Majestus, 59
    golfing, 78
Murder at Cathedral, 111

Nantucket Sleighride, 19
Navy Pilot memorial, 50
New Year's Eve, 96
Nixon, President Richard, inauguration, 34
    request for Moon Rock, 23
Nourse, Joseph, 150

O'Connor, Sandra Day, 94
Oxnam, Bishop Garfield Bromley, 31
Pahlavi, Mohammed Reza (Shah of Iran), 27

Paine, Dr. Thomas, 24
Parkes, Harry, 143
Pelligrini, Ernest, St. Mary's Chapel reredos, 156
    wood carving, 109
Pentagon's cars, 17
Perkins Institute Choir, 27
Perry, Provost Charles, auditorium, 65
    Vietnam Veterans Memorial Service, 145
Pike, Dean James, 31
Plunkett, Patrick, 113
Portable Organ, 45
Price, Fred, 143
Prince Charles, 77
Prince Philip, 90
Prodigal Son, 164

Queen Elizabeth II, Queen Mother Mary's kneeler, 33
    visit, 90
Quoton, Henry, 164

Rare Book Library, exhibit room, 91
    gift of, 20
    planning for, 44
Ratti, Joseph, memorial, 39
Read Herbert, Ambry door, 58
    baptismal font cover, 63
Rood beam, 64

St. Andrews Cathedral, Honolulu, 163
St. Andrews Society, Kirkin' o' the Tartan, 72
St. David's Wales, 162
St. Joan of Arc, 162
St. Paul Statue, 141
Satterlee, Rt. Rev. Henry Yates, interment, 149
    purchase of Nourse estate, 150
Sayre, Very Rev. Francis B., bio, 13-35
    Bricklayer's Union, 68
    building the tower, 45
    cathedral fire, 52
    dedicating font cover, 126
    eight heads, 115
    Frohman-Warneke, 38
    Garth fountain, 55
    General White's funeral, 68
    iconography of bosses, 48
    insulating tower louvers, 106
    light fixtures, 42
    Majestus, 59
    Monjo angels, 49

New Year's Eve, 96
    prayer, 168
    public address speakers, 53
    relations with Tucker, 139
    Washington equestrian statue, 40
    woodworking hobby, 64
Schmidt, Jakob, door hinges, 37
    wrought-iron bishop, 37
Scruggs, Jan, 145
Seferlis, Constantine, Della Robbia Boss, 116
    Helen Keller corbel, 131
    sculpting the eight heads, 115
Semler, Margot, 90
Shands, Anthony, 163
Shankar, Pandit Ravi, 26
Slype, 20
Smith, Captain John, 155
Smith, James, 163
Stones, special memorial, 162
Supreme Court Building, 94
Surveying the nave, 152

Temple Sinai, 30
Thoron, Benjamin, 116
Trevillian, Howard, 136
Tucker, Carl, bio, 124-139
Tucker, Lyn, bio, 124-139

Vergers, label mould terminations, 16
Vietnam Veterans, the Salute to, 145
Volunteers, 165

Walker, Rt. Rev. John T., canon, 67
    interment, 150
Warner, Secretary John, 52
Wheeler, John, 145
White, The Rev. Andrew, 155
White Family, 160
Whitechapel Guild, Old Post Office, 157
    training bell ringers, 143
Wilson, President Woodrow, appointment of
    Lippman, 106
    canopy, 49
    grandfather to Dean Sayre, 13
    interment, 149
Winfield, Rodney, 24

Yellin, Clare, 87
Yellin, Samuel, Children's Chapel, 130

About the Author

ROBERT E. KENDIG, a native Virginian, was educated at the College of William and Mary and at the George Washington University. A career officer in the United States Air Force, he subsequently served as Director of Planning at the University of Maryland for an additional 20 years. He has been a volunteer at the Washington National Cathedral since 1978.

D. DODGE THOMPSON, writer of the Foreword, has been Chief of Exhibitions at the National Gallery of Art since 1980. He received his undergraduate education from the University of Pennsylvania and earned graduate degrees from Harvard and Cambridge Universities.